hello...

We are proud to bring you our tenth edition. The making of this issue began with the theme of 'trails', inspired by Nick Hunt's evocative piece on the introduction of Sámi reindeer to the Scottish Highlands, continuing a story trail that began when Vikings made the same journey with their herds over a thousand years ago (p16). We delve further into the theme in Mack Woodruff's investigation of a deep ocean trail connecting the eastern shores of Japan with the Great Barrier Reef, transporting residual radiation from the Fukushima Daiichi nuclear disaster in 2011 to a fragile ecosystem already on a knife edge (p40).

Both of these stories got us thinking about how we often perceive oceans as separating lands and cultures when perhaps we need to start thinking of them as means of connection. Just as the ongoing pandemic has shown us, the borders and nations we use to understand the world are human constructs that don't translate to nature. The Great Barrier Reef isn't safe from a disaster 'belonging' to Japan, and the ocean isn't a gap between two continents, but a trail leading migrating whales to breeding grounds (p134), or a conveyor belt of plastic that eventually washes up on an island where seabirds breed (p58).

The latter half of the issue was made during lockdown, when the nature of our connectedness was thrown into sharp relief; as was our withdrawal from it. On p114, photographer Jim Marsden reflects on how it feels to pause while Lucy Jones, author of *Losing Eden*, investigates the language we use for the natural world, and how new words and voices are needed now more than ever in the "rubble of the pandemic" (p22).

Since we launched our first edition in 2014, *Ernest* has gathered a loyal readership around the world and it has been a real joy to get to know our community and allow the journal to grow and to evolve. 2020 was going to be a big year for us as we not only celebrated the launch of our tenth edition – a real milestone in independent publishing – but also worked with partners in the travel industry to launch two more *Ernest* 'Editions'. Unfortunately, due to the coronavirus pandemic, all of our partnerships had to be postponed. So we decided to go back to our roots and launch a crowdfunding campaign to help us bring issue 10 to print. You wouldn't be reading this were it not for the overwhelming support of our campaign backers and patrons – and we would like to take this opportunity to convey our heartfelt thanks for your generosity and encouragement during these challenging times. Thanks to your support, we can now look forward to bringing you many more issues over the coming years.

contents

DAN COOK

6 INVENTORY I
A curated assortment of artefacts, inspiring projects and curious tales including botanical cyanotypes, trail teas, ocean tapestries, lunar birds, sacred trees, Sheffield knife crafters and moonlit journeys.

"their antlers sprout like living moss – like reindeer lichen – softly furred." p16

16 MILK OF DEER
From Arctic tundra to the Highlands: how the introduction of reindeer to the Cairngorms has rejuvenated an ancient Scottish herding culture.

22 BEING NATURE
Exploring our language for the natural world, and how new words are needed now more than ever.

30 GASTROPHYSICS
Investigating sensory stimulation in our relationship with food.

36 PLANKTON RECORDER
A steampunk contraption that has been unravelling a marine tapestry for nearly 90 years.

SAM HOSBON

40 OCEAN TRAILS
How the Great Barrier Reef is being affected by the Fukushima nuclear disaster nearly 10 years on.

50 TRAIN DREAMS
Environmentally-conscious travel has been made all the easier with the renaissance of sleeper trains.

58 SEA NOMADS
Meet the seabirders, a group of scientists on the frontline of Britain's gannet study and conservation effort.

70 ROOT BRIDGES
Living architecture grown from the roots of the rubber fig tree.

114 CREATIVE PAUSE
Reflecting on the human need to put down the to-do list.

118 INTO THE UNFATHOMED
Meet the woman who bridged the gap between science and literature.

126 CHASING AURORA
How the thrill of the chase can be just as exciting as the spectacle itself.

134 AN OCEAN ODYSSEY
Surprising oceanic migrations of our largest and smallest creatures.

140 WHAT WOULD GWEN DO?
Photographer Hazel Simcox reveals the literary inspiration behind her mountainscapes.

DAN COOK

exploring islands

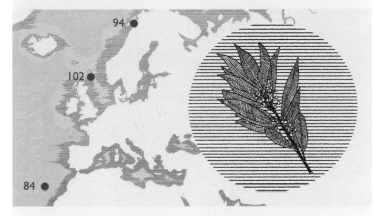

94 ●

102 ●

84 ●

84 ISLE OF ETERNAL SPRING
Subtropical laurel forest | levada walks | Ponta do Pargo lighthouse | The Monte Toboggan Run

94 IN TOWN FOR LOFOTFISKE
Lofoten's fishing season | escaping the elements at Anita's Sjømat | the winter surfers of Unstad

102 POSTCARD FROM THE EDGE
Life on Britain's most remote island | all aboard the Good Shepherd | the knitters of Fair Isle

112 PLAN YOUR ADVENTURE
How to get there | where to stay and eat | island experiences

> "history's heroes are beacons of exertion and doing.
> but where are our heroes of being?" p114

150 INVENTORY II
Learn how to lay and track a scout trail, dive into a wild swimming adventure and seek out the mysterious walking palm with our compendium of knowledge, techniques and kit for a life outdoors.

inventory 1

MICHELLE BURNS, MICHELLEBURNS.ART

CONSERVATION
THE BLACK-THROATED FINCH PROJECT

In 2019 the controversial Adani coal mine in Queensland, Australia was given government approval. This approval will see the opening of one of the world's largest coal mines and lead to the devastation of local flora and fauna and indigenous cultures, as well as increasing global CO_2 emissions. Artist Charlotte Watson decided to respond.

Within the area of the proposed mine lives the diminutive black-throated finch. Its blue-grey head, cinnamon-brown body and black breast has earned it the nickname 'Parson Finch', and numbers have steadily declined to endangered levels. With the opening of the mine the birds' future will be even more uncertain, and extinction ever more likely.

"The plight of the black-throated finch became symbolic for many people in Australia," Charlotte says. "I wanted to give the politicians a piece of my mind, and by that I mean a bit of heart." So Charlotte reached out online, calling out for artwork to highlight the plight of the bird. The project has grown rapidly – to date, more than 1,600 artworks have been sent to key politicians in response to the crisis. Words: **Jim Marsden**. Contribute your own finch art at **charlottewatson.org/black-throated-finch**.

OCEAN TAPESTRY

'Beauty is only possible when it is kind to the environment.' This pearl of wisdom is core to the ethos of many designers and makers of our generation; none more so than Vanessa Barragao, whose stunning work addresses the devastating effects of the textile industry on our coral reefs. Embodying art and activism, Vanessa uses yarns salvaged from the textile industry, and traditional craft techniques such as latch hook, macrame and crochet, to create her large scale ocean floor motifs: a kaleidoscope of colours that contrast starkly with the bleaching of coral in our oceans. Follow her work on Instagram @vanessabarragao_work

Dictyota dichotoma in the young state, & in fruit.

Plocamium coccineum. (in fruit)

CURIOUS HISTORY
TOMES THROUGH TIME

Perusing someone else's bookshelf can feel deliciously voyeuristic, and just as revealing (but not as verboten) as a peek inside their medicine cabinet. But it wasn't so long ago that books were stored in almost every way imaginable except for vertical and spine out. This is an edited extract from *Elements of a Home* by Amy Azzarito, which explores the curious histories of everyday household objects (Chronicle Books, 2020), £14.99. Illustrations: **Alice Pattullo**

Scrolls on shelves
The earliest books had no spines at all – they were scrolls of papyrus. Some readers arranged their collection on shelves fitted with pigeon holes so that the scrolls could be stored flat. Others arranged them so they stood straight up.

Codices in boxes
Composed of papyrus sheets bound in wooden covers, this became the most popular form for presenting text in first-century Europe. Text was copied by hand, and covers sometimes inlaid with jewels. Trunks often had three locks – the keys held by three different people.

PHOTOGRAPHY
BLUE IMPRESSIONS

For *Ernest*, the cyanotype is the perfect embodiment of art and science: a moment frozen in light and shadow, conjured by chemicals in that dreamy cyan blue. While it was Sir John Herschel who developed the cyanotype method, an acquaintance of his, Anna Atkins, put the technique to innovative use – to create blueprints of her vast collection of botanical specimens.

These she collated in her 1843 book, *Photographs of British Algae: Cyanotype Impressions*, the first book to be illustrated by photographs. Anna was already an accomplished illustrator – a hobby considered suitably genteel for women of that period – but being the daughter of a respected scientist at the British Museum opened doors to her that would otherwise have remained closed, allowing her to mix in scientific circles and advance her study of British flora. Even by today's standards her cyanotype impressions – the labels handwritten by Anna – are so detailed and intricate, you can distinguish one species from the next. **Anna Atkins' cyanotypes are part of the Natural History Museum's collection; nhm.ac.uk**

WORKMANSHIP
SHEFFIELD'S 'LITTLE MESTERS'

The cutlers of Sheffield are heartening survivors of another era. Even today, Sheffield-made pocket knives are still produced by apprentice-trained specialists – partly thanks to the city's long tradition of highly skilled craftsmen known as 'little mesters'.

"People who are familiar with the term 'little mester' would call me a modern version," says Michael May, who turns out beautifully finished pocket and kitchen knives from his workshop in a former steel factory. Trained at one of the larger Sheffield firms, Michael is a living link in an ongoing tradition. Tools like his 1930s belt grinder ("solid as the day it was made") were bought from a previous generation of knife makers when they retired, while he himself has a 21-year-old apprentice who's beginning to work more independently.

"In Sheffield's heyday a knife maker could source everything they needed for the job within walking distance," explains Michael, and he still buys local whenever he can. Most of his handle materials come from within Yorkshire, and his fancier Damascus steel blades are forged by a smith in a neighbouring workshop.

His more elaborate knives can involve nearly 60 different processes, and might take him at least a day – and perhaps a drop or two of blood – to make. Handsome they may be, but fundamentally they're still tools designed for hard use. The knife in Michael's own pocket is one that he crafted himself – a classic clip-point 'Barlow' model with ox horn scales. "Made around 12 years ago and still going strong." Words: **Joly Braime**. Pocket knives from £67; **michaelmayknives.com**

Back to the shelf
With the advent of the printing press, the number of books increased. Books in larger collections were chained in place; the chain fixed to the spine. It was not until 1535, when the first printed spine was created, that books spun into the position we're familiar with today.

MOUNTAIN MAPS

One of my favourite childhood books was *Busy, Busy Town* by Richard Scarry. It was full of madcap scenes and exciting cut-aways – a railway station mêlée! A power plant schematic! A hectic intersection – "Look! Mr Rabbit's car's been flattened by a steamroller!!!" But perhaps the best thing about the book was the panoramic maps – transportive bird's eye views of town and country; intricate mazes of visual story.

I experienced the same feeling of eye-popping hyperreality when I opened *The Alps* – a collection of vistas that manage to present iconic alpine features in such a way that they grace the viewer with a kind of omnipresence. Unlike normal maps, where the reader gazes down onto a flattened chart of contours and coded features, here the landscapes unfurl and beckon you in. Again and again I felt as though I were falling into worlds to be explored; the sheer valleys and peaks, following hairpin roads to lilac lakes, catching funiculars from meadow to summit. On one page, I flew over the ravines of Val D'Isarco, then, turning the page, I was surely piloting a microlight over the Rhaetian Alps. Truly immersive, these are IMAX maps.

In his excellent introduction, Tom Dauer notes that alpine panoramas are "not reproductions, but inventions" and it is to the Austrian master, Heinrich C. Berann – a self-described cartographic 'swindler' – that we owe these thrills. From 1956 Berann was assisted in his Innsbruck studio by his pupil Heinz Vielkind. For 40 years they worked together before Vielkind went it alone.

It's easy to overlook panoramic maps yet their ubiquity at ski slopes, city centres and Olympic parks testify to their versatile, expedient beauty. Magical, meticulous inundations of information, this book is an eye-opening alpine tour d'horizon. Words: **Dan Richards**. *The Alps* by Tom Dauer (Thames & Hudson, 2020), £35.

Cima Cad in di
San Lug ano
2839 m

Monte Meduce
2402 m
Croda Rotta
2632 m

Pale di Menotto
2248 m

Croda dei Baranci
2922 m

Rocca dei Baranci
2937 m

Monte Cristallo
3221 m

Monte Civetta
3220 m

Punta Sorapiss
3205 m

Dobbiaco

BOOK
MOONLIGHT TRAVELLERS

In this collaboration between Quentin Blake and Will Self, winged creatures on stilts stalk across otherworldly landscapes by the light of pastel moons. Tantalisingly, not all of the illustrations are fantastical. Among the drawings of men punting across mountainsides on wobbly wheeled frames, there are pictures of what appear to be migrants, humping packs through swamps or adrift on the sea in crowded boats. Extraordinary journeys made by moonlight.
Words: **Joly Braime**. *Moonlight Travellers* by Will Self and Quentin Blake (Thames & Hudson, 2019), £16.95

WILD FOOD
TRAIL TEAS

Longstanding *Ernest* contributor Aidan Meighan illustated these beautiful designs for our Trail Tea enamel mugs, inspired by foraged teas you can make in the great outdoors. From spruce needles to haw berries, why not pluck yourself a few ingredients from nature's larder on your next slow adventure?
Trail Tea mugs, available from mid November, **ernestjournal.co.uk/store**.

Always take a reputable wild food guidebook with you when foraging – if you're not sure, don't pick it.

Spruce needles
Resinous, refreshing and rich in vitamin C – spruce needle tea is the perfect pick-me-up after a long hike. Pick the young needles (they taste sweeter) at the tips of the branches and infuse in hot, not boiling, water. Do not confuse with yew needles – they are toxic.

ORNITHOLOGY
TO THE MOON & BACK

In the 17th century, the English minister and scientist Charles Morton wrote a treatise entitled *Birds in the Moon*, claiming that birds migrated to the moon and back every year, a trip he estimated would take 60 days if the poor birds could maintain a flight speed of 200kmph. He suggested that birds were not affected by gravity or air resistance and that they could complete the journey in two months by sleeping for 'most of the journey', sustained by excess fat. Watching the birds disappear each year into the endless sky, he could see no other solution to their absence than the idea that they must be leaving Earth, asking: "Whither should these creatures go, unless it were to the moon?"

Bird migration is often associated with movements of the sun, the warming and cooling of the seasons, but many species do use the moon to shape their behavioural patterns. A study of monogamous Barau's petrels on the volcanic Réunion Island in the Indian Ocean observed birds travelling to their mating sites over a period of time, and discovered they synchronised their journeys with the full moon, with the increase of moonlight triggering their hunting and mating instincts. In contrast, European storm petrels in Shetland use the cover of darkness to avoid being attacked by skuas and gulls, only returning to their nests in the dead of night. It's an amazing phenomenon, and one that is best enjoyed on the uninhabited island of Mousa, where a colossal Iron Age broch stands empty except for the thousands of storm petrels that swarm into the tower every night. The island is popular among summer visitors, who come to see the petrels returning to their nests by the half-light of the midnight sun. An edited extract from *Dark Skies: A Journey Into the Wild Night*, by Tiffany Francis, new paperback edition (Bloomsbury, 2020), £10.99

Hawthorn berries
Hawthorn is Britain's most abundant hedgerow tree, so you'll not be short of berries for an autumnal brew. They look like mini red apples, and require soaking for 12 hours to soften them before infusing, but all worth it for a tart and tangy tea that's high in antioxidants.

Gorse flowers
The thorny gorse bush flowers at any time of year and is commonly found on clifftops and heathland. Its vivid yellow flowers have a mild coconut and almond flavour – perfect for a calming cup of tea before a night under canvas. Bruise the petals slightly before steeping.

Birch twig
Easily identified by its peeling white bark, the silver birch can be found in woods all over Britain. Birch twigs and buds have diuretic properties, so are good for flushing out toxins. Make sure the water isn't boiling, as that will evaporate the wintergreen flavour.

GEOGRAPHY
ISLAND DREAMS

"Of the islands I've cherished most, I met many first in print." In *Island Dreams*, Gavin Francis examines our collective fascination with islands. In this edited extract, he follows the literature of Charles Darwin, Bruce Chatwin and Herman Melville to remote islands in the Pacific and Southern Atlantic Ocean.
Island Dreams: Mapping an Obsession, by Gavin Francis (Canongate, 2020), £20

Chiloé
This island is notorious for a macabre mythology in which much of the population is said to still believe: goblins, warlocks and all manner of creatures are thought to populate the caves in the forest along the eastern shore. When Darwin visited in the 1830s there were tales of people accused of devil-worship being sent to the Inquisition in Lima. On the western coast, I watched the Pacific – the roar of it, the mother of all oceans, deadened all other sounds.

Tierra del Fuego
In my youth I was captivated by E. Lucas Bridges' *The Uttermost Part of the Earth* – a book about growing up on Tierra del Fuego, at the tip of Patagonia. I went there aged 26, between a spell training in medicine and taking a job as a doctor with the British Antarctic Survey. I travelled north to the Valle Carbajal. A Fuegian fox ran off with my bread rolls, and at the summit I swung my legs over glaciers the colour of petrified sky.

Bird Island, South Georgia
I took a 'tender' to meet scientists who live year-round on Bird Island – a splinter of rock off South Georgia's western cape. They handed me a broom handle 'seal-bodger' with which to beat off any fur seals that approached with fangs bared. Black-browed albatrosses nested along the slopes. Up on the plateau I tiptoed, awe-struck, between their nests. These immense birds with a 12ft wingspan were untroubled by my presence.

DENDROLOGY
THE PŌHUTUKAWA ▶

Trees have long been important to us, not just for their beauty and character, but also because they have been central to our existence. They supply many of the vital ingredients for life – food, medicine, timber – and also ecological services such as providing the oxygen we breathe, controlling soil erosion, trapping pollution, acting as carbon sinks and increasing water purity, as well as moderating the climate. Trees have also been the subjects of song, poetry, stories and art, and are woven into our religions, folklore and customs.

In November and December – which is of course summer in the southern hemisphere – the Pōhutukawa tree puts on the most striking display of red flowers. They can be so abundant that from a distance trees almost look as if they are on fire. Endemic to New Zealand, it grows mainly in coastal forests, where it flourishes in the warm conditions, but can withstand ocean winds and salt spray; the Māori name, Pōhutukawa, means 'sprinkled with spray'.

Pōhutukawa has a great cultural significance for New Zealanders. In Māori mythology a warrior called Tawhaki set out to avenge his father's death. He travelled to the heavens to ask for help, but fell to Earth and died. The red flowers of Pōhutukawa represent his spilled blood.

The Māori use the tree for boatbuilding, carvings, and in traditional medicine. They believe that when they die their spirit travels to a sacred Pōhutukawa tree (reputed to be over 600 years old) near Cape Reinga at the tip of the North Island. Here they travel along the roots to a cave and then on to the spirit world. The Cape is where the Tasman Sea meets the Pacific, and is seen as the final stepping off point from this world. An edited extract from *Remarkable Trees*, by Christina Harrison and Tony Kirkham, (University of Chicago Press, 2019) £24.95

LIBRARY, ART & ARCHIVES COLLECTION © THE BOARD OF TRUSTEES OF THE ROYAL BOTANIC GARDENS, KEW

milk of deer

When a pair of Swedish newlyweds introduced reindeer to the
Cairngorms after seeing striking parallels between the Highlands and
their native homeland, little did they realise they were rejuvenating
a Scottish herding culture that goes back to the Ice Age

WORDS: **NICK HUNT**
ILLUSTRATIONS: **RUTH THORP**

They crossed the North Sea by ship, just like the
Vikings did. At first there were only eight of them,
four females and four males. The wind was strong,
the seas were high; by the time they reached the east
coast of Scotland they were weak and ill, and one of
them had accidentally gored their herder in the eye so
that he arrived wearing a piratical-looking eyepatch.
Another died during the herd's month or so in
quarantine. The survivors were transported north to
colonise a new land.

At first they made themselves at home among the
gnarled Scots pines of Rothiemurchus, a remnant of
the once-great Caledonian Forest, 9,000 years old, that
blanketed the north of Britain after the glaciers melted.
The settlement period was hard – their lives made a
misery by tormenting midgies, horseflies and mosquitoes
they could do nothing to escape – but the colony was
strengthened by a second wave of pioneers, followed by
a third, a fourth. Winter brought the snow they loved.
Soon the reindeer gained their freedom.

The fences were taken down. Beyond the woods
lay mountains. Ahead of them, and above, stretched
hundreds of square miles of eroded granite peaks,
straths (shallow riverine valleys), lairigs (deep glacial
passes), clear-flowing rivers, burns and lochs, and

flora they would have known from their homeland
in Scandinavia: a landscape swathed in a squelching
weave of sphagnum moss, fork-moss, crimson
rustwort, lichens, ferns, monster pawwort, blaeberry
and tough montane grass, the only patch of Arctic
tundra that exists in Britain. And most importantly
of all, an intricate dendritic form of the palest green
that resembles nothing so much as a diagram of a
nervous system, growing simply everywhere: reindeer
lichen, a crucial part of the new arrivals' diet.

These reindeer in Scotland owe their existence
to a honeymoon. Two years after the Second World
War ended, the newly married Dr Ethel Lindgren,
a Swedish-American anthropologist, and Mikel Utsi,
a Swedish Sámi reindeer herder, arrived by train
at the eastern edge of the Cairngorms mountain
range. "Looking across Rothiemurchus Forest to the
Cairngorms from the railway bridge at Aviemore on a
cold morning in April 1947," Utsi later recalled, "I was
instantly reminded of reindeer pastures in Lapland…
species of ground, rock and tree lichens, which are
elsewhere the chief food of reindeer, were plentiful and
of little use to other animals." The similarity to his home
– geologically, ecologically and even climatologically
(the lowest temperature ever recorded in Britain, minus

27.2°C, has twice been measured in nearby Braemar) – was what gave him the idea. The newlyweds decided to try breeding reindeer in Scotland.

It took five years, but, using formidable powers of persuasion – Dr Lindgren in particular had an impressive contacts list – they had won the support of the Ministry of Agriculture and the Forestry Commission, which granted them land to use as an experimental enclosure. Utsi personally accompanied those initial eight individuals on the SS *Sarek*, enduring an antler in the eye during the crossing.

Seven decades later, the Cairngorms are home to Britain's only free-living reindeer herd, with around 150 scattered across the plateau. Being free to roam, they can escape the insects that plague them at lower altitude, and – despite the chomping mouths and the slow-growing nature of the plant – the lichen appears no less plentiful than it was in Utsi's day. The herder died in 1979, then Dr Lindgren in 1988, so today's herd is managed by Tilly and Alan Smith. Tilly came to Scotland originally to work as a volunteer. "I was struck by the beauty of the landscape," she told me, "the endearing nature of the reindeer and the reindeer keeper (Alan) wasn't bad looking! The rest is history."

A WORLD CONTENDER

The experiment has been so successful that, at the World Reindeer Herders Congress held in northeast China in 2013, the Smiths – alongside Sámis, Soyots, Inuits, Evenks, Chukchis, Komis, Nenets, Iñupiaqs and other herding cultures from around the globe – accepted Scotland's recognition as the 13th member. "I have been to congresses in Tromsø, Kautokeino, Jokkmokk and also a council meeting in Salekhard, on the Yamal Peninsula," says Tilly. "You never know, one day the congress may be held in Scotland."

This seemingly random string of events – the chance honeymoon of two Swedes that eventually led to Scotland's ascension to a cervine community that spans the Northern Hemisphere – may sound bizarre, at first. But the story of reindeer in the Cairngorms is older than the 1950s.

You can glimpse them in paleontology: middens of antlers and butchered bones have been unearthed

"you can glimpse them in paleontology: middens of antlers and butchered bones have been unearthed"

throughout Scotland. As the glaciers of the Ice Age retreated, leaving the straths and lairigs behind – and as the first birches and pines of the future Caledonian Forest took root in the thawing permafrost – Paleolithic hunting groups migrated northwards into new lands, like people cautiously setting forth on a recently drained seabed. They were following reindeer herds, which roamed throughout northern Europe. As the ice melted and the sea levels rose, severing Britain from the Continent, both the reindeer and their hunters were islanded, cut off from larger seasonal patterns of migration. We know little about the relationship between humans and reindeer in that time, but it seems likely that – in common with other animist cultures – these beautiful animals would have found themselves objects of worship.

Whether they were semi-domesticated, like their cousins in Scandinavia – selectively bred for their meat, milk and wondrous warm pelts – is another unknown, lost in prehistory. But we do have hints and clues, distorted through centuries of myth. 'On milk of deer I was reared / On milk of deer I was nurtured', goes the Highlands lullaby *Bainne nam Fiadh* (Milk of Deer);

perhaps nonsense, or perhaps an echo from before recorded time. Regarded as fairy cattle, deer appear in folk-tales along with their supernatural wards, especially in stories involving the Cailleach. In Celtic mythology the Cailleach is the 'divine hag' and Queen of Winter, the touch of whose staff freezes the ground. She might also be glimpsed on cold nights milking her herd of magic deer.

TRAVELLING TALES

Are these stories evidence of an ancient Scottish herding culture, one that was supplanted, perhaps, by subsequent waves of invasion? Or do they point – as one theory suggests – to a migration not of people but of oral history? When the Vikings settled in Scotland, they may have brought stories of the Sámi tribes with whom they had coexisted, fought and traded within the northern reaches of their homeland, a mysterious reindeer-milking folk who lived at the edge of the world. They might have whispered tales of shamans with magical powers of flight, who journeyed between the worlds to the rhythm of reindeer-skin drums; reindeer urine, suffused with psilocybin from fly agaric mushrooms, was drunk for its hallucinogenic and visionary effects (and, in the centuries to come, stories of flying reindeer might have been the origin not only of airborne witches but of Father Christmas's sleigh).

Whether reindeer were herded or merely hunted, by the landing of the SS *Sarek* they had been absent from Scotland for centuries, if not millennia. When did the last of them disappear? No one really knows. Vikings enter the story again with a single intriguing line from *The Orkneyinga Saga*, written by the Earls of Orkney, describing a reindeer hunt in Caithness in the 13th century. Some scholars take this as proof of their survival into medieval times; others claim that the line actually refers to red deer, and that reindeer went extinct in Britain – as they did across Germany, Denmark and southern Scandinavia – 10,000 years earlier. They have now been home for 70 years. Did the reindeer lichen miss them?

It is a grey day in January, unseasonably mild. My friend Dougie and I are walking to Strath Nethy. It is my first morning in the Cairngorms and my heart aches for

"their pelts are white, silver, grey, dun, minutely flecked with black, and snowy ruffs sway around their necks as they stoop to graze"

snow, but there is only bitter rain. The mountains are sodden and purple-brown. Then, across the little stream, appear five reindeer.

In his years of walking these mountains, Dougie has never seen them before. Together we stand silently and watch them watching us. Their pelts are white, silver, grey, dun, minutely flecked with black, and snowy ruffs sway around their necks as they stoop to graze. Their antlers sprout like living moss – like reindeer lichen – softly furred. Their sensitive noses twitch. I do not know the stories yet – I am yet to hear the names of Utsi, Lindgren or the Smiths, or folk-songs about milk of deer, or Sámi shamans, Viking earls or the winter-bringing Cailleach – and all I can think about is how beautiful they look, how right they look, standing there in the midst of Scotland's tundra.

The spell only lasts for a minute or two. We have miles to walk today and perhaps the reindeer do as well. We take the path beside the stream and they turn the other way. Minutes after they have gone, it begins to snow. ●

being nature

Lucy Jones, author of *Losing Eden*, investigates the language we use about the natural world and how new words and voices are needed in the rubble of the pandemic

WORDS: **LUCY JONES**
PHOTOS: **SAM HOBSON**

my book *Losing Eden: Why Our Minds Need the Wild* started as an attempt to answer a question that seems quite simple on the face of it: how and why does spending time in natural places affect our mental and emotional health?

But of course, the question soon flipped. As I reconnected with nature, through walking on Walthamstow Marshes in London during a period of recovery from illness, I realised how disconnected I was, how little I knew about the processes around me, the other species with whom we share the earth, and then, more worryingly, how much nature we have lost and are losing. It was bittersweet. On the one hand, the coots and the kestrels, the tansy and the trees, the swims

in rivers and freezing cold seas, gave me something profound: a sense of calm, soothing, even sanity. On the other, I began to experience what Aldo Leopold described so well: "One of the penalties of an ecological education is that one lives ... in a world of wounds."

I started to wonder; how, then, does our modern-day estrangement from the living world affect our minds? As I studied these questions, it seemed that one of the problems we currently face is the words that we use about the natural world. Our winnowing relationship is mirrored in our thin linguistics.

'Natural capital', for example, the term used by the British government to refer to the wealth and value of ecosystem services is horrible and highlights an attitude that needs to change: that nature is only worth something if it is giving us dividends. 'The' environment rather than 'our' environment underlines the misconception that we live on some kind of separate planet, that we are somehow not alive because of the living world around us.

Even the most beautiful natural areas of England are given extremely boring names that make you switch off as soon as you hear them. The marshes near my then London home, which was a multi-sensory wonder-park, from the sounds of water voles plopping into the River Lea to the taste of blackberries and the smell of tansy, was officially called an SSSI, a Site of Special Scientific Interest. Are you still with me? The ugly acronym just doesn't do the place justice.

POOR CHOICE OF WORDS

I'm starting to wonder about the big cheese of them all. The word we all use, because it is useful and easy: nature. I'm wondering if describing the rest of the living world as 'nature' is unhelpful and problematic. We are part of nature even if we don't think we are, or accept we are, so in a way it solidifies the separation between people and the rest of the living world. The blanket term 'nature', meaning what is out there, not us, the other stuff that's alive, allows us to wallow in this hallucination that we are not stitched into the world as we truly are. In fact, we are entangled with the rest of nature, not just for the air we breathe, the water we drink and the food we eat, but in other ways, as has become only too clear in the COVID-19 pandemic.

Most people today probably wouldn't hold the opinion that was common for centuries that all species were created to serve man's purpose. I doubt anyone holds the old belief that horseflies were created so people could exercise their wits against them. (And I'm not just saying this as someone with a swollen cleg bite on my calf).

But it seems the mainstream view is still that man is superior and deserves much, much more than 'nature', which is out there.

Language matters. We can see it in the way Latin terminology superseded colloquial names for flowers and plants, which were filled with human symbolism and emotional experience. Don't we lose something when we no longer have terms like 'cheese-bob' for woodlouse, or 'devil's rings' for caterpillar or 'bum towel'

for long-tailed tits, in our vernacular? Perhaps this moment was the beginning of our current epidemic of plant-blindness, when, today, the majority of people can't recognise an oak.

How we talk about introduced species matters, too. "When you hear about the problems caused by a 'non-native and invasive' plant species, I urge you to find out how that plant found its way to these shores and interrogate the heavy language you use to describe where it came from and how it grows," wrote organic grower Claire Ratinon about the importance of knowing the colonial history behind the vocabulary around plants.

> "we are entangled with the rest of nature, not just for the air we breathe, the water we drink & the food we eat"

Concurrently, many people have images of naturalness in their minds of what, for example, a wildflower meadow should look like, influenced by seed boxes sold for aesthetic value rather than biodiversity. In a biodiversity crisis, how important is aesthetic planting instead of planting for habitats and pollen for insects in free-fall? Our perceptions of nature are subject to 'shifting baseline syndrome', meaning a gradual change in accepted norms of how a natural environment should look. For my grandmother, it was normal for her to grow up around great-crested newts and clouds of insects. I have never seen a great-crested newt nor a 'moth snowstorm' on car headlights since early childhood.

Lockdown has shown starkly the inequality of access to the natural world in Britain. It makes a mockery of the blanket idea of 'nature'. For some people, access to 'nature' will mean a municipal bedding plant on a roundabout. For others, it will mean a large, biodiverse meadow. For others, 'nature', the countryside, feels unwelcome and hostile as potential places of prejudiced encounters. Just as people are heterogeneous, so our perceptions of nature are, too. If we had a fuller, richer lexicon to speak about what we really mean, an ecological education, essentially, perhaps we would be able to see the problem of ecological collapse and eco-alienation more clearly.

"this is an opportunity for re-writing our dysfunctional relationship with the natural world"

The word 'wild' is an interesting, nebulous one. Today, it is a fashionable concept in the industrialised West. It's the name of a festival in England, a health fruit bar and an IPA beer. My book is one of many published at the moment with the word 'wild' in the title.

But in Britain today, the Cairngorms are perhaps the only landscape that would be vaguely similar to the wilderness of days gone by. Much of the rest of the countryside has been razed and cleared into land for agriculture or housing. However, we remain under its spell. In the last few years, there's been an expansion of interest in rewilding, 'wild swimming', 'wild camping', wild child-rearing and films about wild experience.

We are drawn to the wild, even if we've never truly experienced it. As it is now minimal, interpretations can be manifold.

My three-year-old, who spends plenty of time in the woods, and has a mother who is very keen on her not being limited by cultural ideas of the rest of nature, said the other day, "I don't like wild woods; I just like nature." The separation of scary nature from safe nature begins! Perhaps the idea of the 'wild' meets the need for the 'wolf in the woods' that's baked into our genes, despite living in a country shorn of its apex predators.

Apart from trips to the Sinai desert and the icy tundra of Svalbard for *Losing Eden*, I find wildness closer to home. I felt wild yesterday when I swam in an icy cold river. When I'd warmed up, I wallowed in the shallows, lolling towards the muddy banks to inspect the underside of leaves for ladybird larvae and butterfly eggs.

A CHANCE TO RESET

The middle of 2020 feels like a liminal space. A time when containers are breaking down, and change is possible. It is in the rubble of the pandemic, which has tipped normality upside down for so many, as well as in new-found consciousness and empathy around issues of inequality, ecocide and structural racism, that we might be able to find new words. At the moment, in so many arenas, the words we currently have seem inadequate.

This is an opportunity for re-writing our dysfunctional relationship with the natural world, for seeing the full messy grossness and terrible awe of nature in its unfettered entirety. I don't want my perception of the countryside to be limited by the frames of the 18th-century Romantic poets anymore. New words and voices are needed alongside a new value system, centred on the thriving of all life.

How do we define nature? I think our current inherited ideas can be weirdly flat: of perfect lawns, pretty flowers, neatness and tidiness, England's green and pleasant land. But really nature isn't pleasant. It's dynamic, full of processes, of becoming, of eating, the "universal chomp", as Annie Dillard puts it. It's defined by élan and brio and energy and teeth and claws. It's wild. So, I'll start. I'm going to suggest that instead of 'nature', perhaps we should simply use... 'life'? ●

Losing Eden: Why Our Minds Need the Wild was published by Allen Lane in February 2020.

Andanza

When Sarah Beseler first moved to Madrid 25 years ago, she longed for green landscapes. Over time, her craving morphed into a profound connection with the rugged beauty and tranquility of northern Spain. A seasoned traveller who has crafted itineraries across the continents, Sarah launched Andanza Travel to enable others to share in her enchantment with this unspoilt region on her doorstep.

Nourished by a cool, maritime climate, Galicia is renowned for its green vistas and unique cuisine, combining the freshest seafood with hearty stews: think melt-in-your-mouth octopus drizzled in paprika and olive oil, and fried *Padrón* peppers sprinkled with rock salt. Here you can hike fjord-like inlets, sail to remote Atlantic islands or sample Albariño wine on a vineyard tour.

Asturias nestles between the Atlantic Ocean and the Cantabrian mountain range, its coastline dotted with charming fishing villages. Barely 20km inland, the chiselled summits of the Picos de Europa soar to 2,600 metres, its slopes home to deer, bears and wolves. A day can include learning to surf on wild beaches or abseiling down river gorges, then winding down the evening in a fine restaurant, sampling the best local dishes from a six-course tasting menu.

Further east, Cantabria offers an astounding variety of landscapes, from pristine beaches to the Valles Pasiegos, an area of lush green hills where farmers still pick their crops with traditional *cuévano* wicker baskets on their backs. Spend your day exploring prehistoric caves, then a warren of medieval cobbled streets in Santillana del Mar, before heading to the vibrant waterfront of Santander with its startlingly modernist cultural centre.

Having thoroughly immersed herself in the culture, cuisine and 'joie de vivre' of the Spanish people, Sarah is ideally placed to share her insight. Simply decide on the flavour of your trip and she will build you a bespoke itinerary – staying at handpicked, elegant hotels and allowing you to explore the majestic scenery of northern Spain at your own pace and away from the crowds.

Andanza, by the way, means adventure, travels, wanderings.
Start your journey at andanzatravel.es

GASTRO PHYSICS

You're cruising at 31,000 feet. The drinks trolley beetles past and before you think about it, you've ordered a Bloody Mary – a slightly off-piste choice but one you are craving all the same. As you take your first sip of the salty drink, you look around only to discover how many of your fellow passengers have opted for the same unusual beverage. **Kate Tighe** talks to leading gastrophysicist **Professor Charles Spence** about the quirks of this new field of food-related psychological interest.

ILLUSTRATIONS: **ADAM HOWLING**

If you can believe it, there once was a time when food and science were thought to be completely unrelated. Scientists did their thing in the labs while chefs sat in the kitchen scrambling eggs, both believing that one had nothing to do with the other. It wasn't until Professor Charles Spence, known for his cross-disciplinary approach and scientific rigor, met experimental chef Heston Blumenthal that the lab, kitchen and mind of the diner truly became one.

Aided by Spence and a roster of founding fathers before him, such as Harold McGee, Ferran Adria and Nicholas Kurti, an entirely new and fully formed field of scientific interest, which revolves around food and our experience of it, was born. How we eat and what we like is not simply ruled by our stomach but by our eyes, ears, nose, gut and, most importantly, brain. Gastrophysics is the reason why some food experiences are so powerful and the reason we may be tricked into staying longer in a bar or buying more at a shop. Further than that, it can tell us why The Fat Duck's pink smoked salmon ice cream was so disconcerting to its customers, and can also help us to describe and understand the endless multisensory experience of tasting food and drink.

Gastrophysics, in short, teaches us that the pleasure (or conversely displeasure) we obtain from food is much more complex than we initially imagined – relying on subjective stimuli such as memory, mental associations and even emotion. I spoke to Professor Spence to discuss the exciting research being conducted in this expanding culinary and scientific field.

Charles, how do our surroundings dictate how we experience food?

Well, for a start, the decorations set a certain expectation about the kind of food we are likely to receive. All the way from the 'white cube' mentality of white tablecloths, white walls, no paintings, no music, just a silent respect of the chef's dishes; through to those organic or nature-inspired venues where the fresh produce is on display to elicit natural expectations. Whatever we eat, whenever we eat, there are always surroundings that subtly influence our expectations and the tasting experience that follows.

Can music affect our experience, too?

Music affects us in any number of ways. Perhaps the simplest is the fact that the more we like what we're listening to, the more we enjoy what we're tasting – this is a phenomenon known as 'sensation transference'. As many a bar or restaurant knows only too well, those listening to loud, fast music drink more and often leave sooner to allow other covers in. Something really exciting for my collaborators and I is what's known as 'sonic seasoning' – this is where the music or soundscapes we hear can bias our perception of the taste of the food and drink.

Tell me more about sonic seasoning, please!

There is music or soundscapes that can add sweetness, sourness, bitterness, creaminess and even spiciness to our tasting experience. We associate high-pitched sounds with sweet tastes and low-pitched sounds with bitter tastes. In fact, we recently created musical menus for the kinds of sound properties that are associated with, and accentuate, a range of different tastes. Often, we pick examples of pre-recorded music that has the appropriate sonic qualities, or we work with sound designers, composers and DJs to create new music tracks with the

❝ HOW WE EAT & WHAT WE LIKE IS NOT SIMPLY RULED BY OUR STOMACH BUT BY OUR EYES, EARS, NOSE, GUT &, MOST IMPORTANTLY, BRAIN❞

appropriate qualities. This has produced one of the most surprising results we have come across over the years, and the most counterintuitive. It is so much fun to play with, and to try to convince people of what might, at first, sound preposterous.

What about the sound of food itself or its packaging?
I am convinced that the sonic attributes of packaging sounds can influence us as much as their visual appearance or weight. It is no coincidence that noisy foods, such as crisps, are packaged in a noisy, crinkly bag. We've also conducted research showing that those who hear a cork pop rate a glass of wine as tasting better than those who hear a screw-top bottle being opened instead. On the negative side, just think how your expectations can be deflated by hearing the ding of the microwave from the kitchen when dining at a fancy restaurant.

In your book you say that gastrophysics is very much ruled by 'expectations management'…
Expectations management is the idea that before we taste anything we nearly always have an expectation about what it is we're about to taste. This can come from brand, price, location, appearance or description, for instance, but it is always there. The only exception perhaps is when we go out to eat at a dine-in-the-dark restaurant – but that isn't exactly an everyday eating experience. Nor, suggests the research, is it especially enjoyable from a culinary perspective either.

Is there science to back this up?
Yes, the research suggests that when we actually taste a food we may compare our tasting experience to our expectation, and if there isn't much difference we live in the world of our expectations. This is why it is so

❝ UMAMI, ONE OF THE KEY TASTES IN TOMATO JUICE, & BLOODY MARY GIVEN THE WORCESTER SAUCE, IS PERCEIVED BETTER WHEN PEOPLE LISTEN TO THE LOUD NOISE OF THE AIRPLANE ENGINES ❞

66 WE ARE WORKING ON HOW TO MAKE INSECTS DESIRABLE AS A FOOD SOURCE, & SHIFTING PEOPLE TO OTHER MORE POTENTIALLY SUSTAINABLE FOOD SOURCES SUCH AS JELLYFISH 99

important to manage our expectations effectively. Ideally, I think we want our expectations to be a little better than the experience itself. If the difference gets too great, then we are likely to rebound in what is known as a 'disconfirmation of expectation' response.

One of my favourite examples of this comes from the pink ice cream that was once served in one of the world's top restaurants, The Fat Duck. The chef, Heston Blumenthal, thought the dish had been perfectly seasoned, but the first guests to trial the dish thought it tasted way too salty. In this case, the answer turned out to be that the diners saw a pink ice cream and immediately thought of strawberry (i.e. sweet). In fact, the dish was a frozen crab bisque or smoked salmon ice cream – so the colour was perfectly natural, but the taste was just not what people expected. This led to a disconfirmation of expectation response, and the diners didn't like the dish.

So, why on Earth do we crave tomato juice on airplanes?
I travel a lot for work and often watch the drinks trolley coming down towards the back of the plane. I am struck by how popular Bloody Marys are. Survey results have revealed that a quarter of the population would only think of ordering one of these drinks in the air, while never doing so when they are on the ground.

In 2014, together with a couple of colleagues, we suggested that people might be self-medicating while in the air, by picking a drink that stands up to the unusual sensory environment at altitude. The following year, researchers from Cornell University showed that umami, one of the key tastes in tomato juice, and Bloody Mary given the Worcester sauce, is perceived better when people listen to the loud noise of the airplane engines.

By contrast, sweetness – and in some studies, saltiness too – tend to be depressed by such loud noise. This is part of the reason why plane food is so unhealthy. They have to add 20-30 per cent more salt or sugar in the air to get the same taste that you would on the ground. And it isn't just the noise – the dry air and lowered cabin air pressure also play a part.

Where do you see your research going next?
There is one strand of thinking about how ubiquitous digital technology – smartphones and tablet computers – can be repositioned to enhance the dining experience. For example, it turns out that the colour of the plate affects the taste of the food, but the best colour seems to depend on its contrast with the food you are eating. So rather than buying a rainbow assortment of plate colours, one could eat off a digital tablet and have the screen colour change to optimize the appearance of the food. Some tablets are waterproof, so you might be able to put them in the dishwasher afterwards!

Alongside pursuing the possibilities offered by technology at the table, we're also working on how to make insects desirable as a food source, and how to shift people to other more potentially sustainable food sources, such as jellyfish.

Gastrophysics: The New Science of Eating by Professor Charles Spence (2018) is published by Penguin.

The Continuous Plankton Recorder

This contraption has been compiling a marine tapestry since 1931, and now, according to **Russell Arnott**, provides a unique insight into our plastic addiction and the health of our oceans

The North Sea herring fisheries provided a crucial and plentiful source of cheap protein for post-war Britain in the 1920s. Based in Lowestoft, a young marine biologist named Alister Hardy (*pictured below*) was tasked with predicting where the herring schooled; a conundrum that had evaded even the best fishery scientists. Instead of focusing on the fish, Hardy concentrated on the herrings' food source: microscopic zooplankton. But in order to get a better idea of how this plankton varied across vast areas of the ocean, Hardy had to think outside the box.

Spurred on by a survey to Antarctica on board the RRS *Discovery*, Hardy developed the Continuous Plankton Recorder (CPR). Part steampunk, part Heath Robinson, the torpedo-shaped contraption was designed to be towed behind a vessel, trapping samples of plankton along the way for later analysis. Quickly recognising the expense of conducting surveys on board scientific vessels, Hardy made use of 'ships of opportunity'; commercial cargo ships working their way across established shipping channels. With the first tow in 1931, the CPR has since covered almost 8 million miles using over 250 different ships, making it one of the most expansive biological datasets in the world.

In its 86 years of operation, the science behind the survey has changed very little. Once deployed, planktonic organisms enter the CPR via an aperture at the front. Inside, two reels of silk are dispensed, sandwiching the plankton between them before winding on into a reservoir of formalin, preserving the organisms for later analysis. The rate at which the silk is dispensed is governed by an ingenious impeller mechanism; as the ship goes faster, the impeller spins more rapidly, paying out silk at a faster rate.

With the journey complete, the CPR is recovered, the silk reel is removed and then sent to the Marine Biological Association in Plymouth, Devon. Once there, mile after mile of silk is unravelled by the team of marine taxonomists, who painstakingly identify and count the hundreds of different species of phytoplankton and zooplankton.

Enduring funding cuts and a world war, the survey is now paying off in unexpected ways. Having records that span more than 80 years allows us to observe long-term trends in plankton populations. Our ocean has absorbed a quarter of the excess carbon dioxide we've pumped into our atmosphere, and as tiny indicators of a warmer and more acidic ocean, understanding plankton populations is crucial in modelling how our climate continues to change.

The CPR records also give an insight into the evolution of our plastic addiction. First an entanglement in fishing gear in 1957. Then a stray plastic bag in 1965. Today, up to four per cent of each tow is comprised of stray fishing line and microplastic fragments. In a world where things are increasingly disposable, thankfully the Continuous Plankton Recorder is here to stay. ●

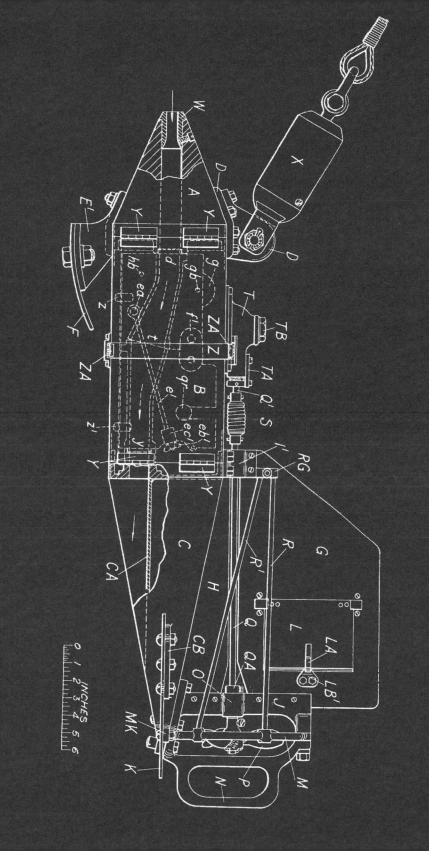

INCHES
0 1 2 3 4 5 6

JUNIPER RIDGE

We formulate Wilderness Perfume by distilling and extracting fragrance from
wildflowers, plants, bark, moss, mushrooms and tree trimmings that we harvest on
the trail. All of our products are named for the wild places they come from.
Our company is built on the simple idea that nothing smells better than the forest and
that the only way to bring this beauty home is to strap on your boots and go there.

HARVEST

If it comes from nature, it is going to change. Unlike synthetic fragrances,
these wilderness perfumes are extracted from real, native-plant sources.

PROCESS

We conceive of our fragrances throughout the West, on dirt roads and
trails, around campfires, and formulate them in our Oakland, California
workshop. All to capture the beauty of the Mojave Desert at sunrise; a thick
blanket of fog draping the wildflower gardens of Big Sur, or a late-season,
sun-baked, snow-carved, glacial canyon high in the Sierra Nevada.

FORMULATION

All Juniper Ridge products are 100% natural and produced using
old perfume making techniques, including distillation, tincturing, infusion
and enfleurage. A hundred years ago, all perfumes were made this way.
These formulas vary from year to year and harvest to harvest,
based on rainfall, temperature, harvesting location, and season.
The exact formula depends on what we find in the wild,
a conversation with the living, wild ecology.

juniperridge.com

ocean trails

The 2011 Fukushima Daiichi nuclear disaster has long been out of the headlines but its devastating legacy is still having a domino effect, as radiation travels on deep ocean currents to new parts of the world – including the fragile ecosystem of the Great Barrier Reef. Australian naturalist **Paul O'Dowd** is closely monitoring this invisible enemy, with the goal of sounding the alarm when disaster eventually strikes.

WORDS & PHOTOS: **MACK WOODRUFF**

▼ Descending to the reef.
▶ Paul taking sand samples
for microplastic testing.

Like so many things in life, trails can be a force for connection, or an avenue towards destruction. In many cases, trails take us inside nature; they connect communities, and form trade routes and roads for ease of movement. But in other contexts, trails can be detrimental. They can facilitate the pillaging of critical resources, or give poachers access to endangered species or pristine tracts of land.

In the Great Barrier Reef, ocean trails are hastening the devastation of this critical natural wonder. Radiation and microplastics from distant regions of the world are brought to its doorstep by a variety of ocean conveyor belts. The 2011 Fukushima Daiichi nuclear disaster has long been out of the headlines, but the devastating legacy is still having a domino effect.

Ocean currents are much slower than air currents, and don't have natural boundaries like trails on land. Ocean trails ebb and flow, they meander and slowly disperse whatever has entered its grip without prejudice: nutrients, plastic, plankton, or radiation – it doesn't matter.

In Port Douglas – a picturesque Queensland coastal village nestled in the foothills of the Daintree rainforest, surrounded by sugar cane fields, lush cow pastures and thick mangrove forests – Australian naturalist Paul O'Dowd is closely monitoring a few of these invisible enemies, with the goal of sounding the alarm when disaster does eventually strike.

As I pull into Paul's driveway, he's already waiting for me outside his front door in the unrelenting Queensland sun, and he greets me with a warm smile. His house is chock-full of an eclectic collection of microscopes, Geiger counters, beakers and sand sifters. Not to mention his cabinet of highly radioactive rocks, an unfinished airplane in his garage and a 30-person bus parked in his backyard as an escape vehicle.

After just a few minutes of talking to Paul, it's impossible to not feel inspired. He humbly prefers to be referred to as a "naturalist" because he isn't a card-carrying marine biologist, but you'd be hard-pressed to find someone who knows more about what's going on in Australia's coastal waters.

Paul and I have known each other since early 2019, when we met on an expedition to Papua New Guinea. Fluent in Pidgin, he's been traveling to the rugged island nation for more than 30 years, pioneering new scuba dive sites and accompanying film crews through some of the thickest jungle on Earth. If you look past his unconventional path and his lack of state-of-the-art equipment, you find a man who is passionately committed to saving our oceans.

FINDING A BASELINE FOR 'NORMAL'

The radiation from the Fukushima disaster in 2011 quickly travelled through air and water to the west coast of North America, but what most didn't know is that it was simultaneously making its way to the Southern Hemisphere via a deep ocean current. These deep ocean flows are slow-moving and more diluted, but the threat that they pose to the Great Barrier Reef is very real.

"What we have here is the canary in the coal mine for this entire impending disaster," Paul says as he holds his Geiger counter up to a mop of brown seaweed washed up on the beach. He hypothesises that the radiation will hit northern Australia's shores in three to five years. Working alone, he's frantically testing radiation levels in seaweed, which he says is "a great bio-accumulator of heavy metals".

The effects of that radiation are relatively unknown. "It could have a similar effect to the ones documented in the Pacific Northwest, with increased rates of mutated fish and growth anomalies," he says. But, perhaps somewhat optimistically, Paul claims, "It could also potentially increase the likelihood of a mutation in coral, giving it an advantage in a warming and acidifying sea." After three massive bleaching events in the past seven years, radiation damage would add insult to injury to the already ailing Great Barrier Reef.

The goal of Paul's radiation monitoring isn't to uncover a massive unfolding problem, it's to establish a baseline of what 'normal' looks like. Most things on this planet have some sort of radioactivity, so it's vital to establish the normal readings to know when a dangerous uptick occurs.

"You can see from the spaced out clicks on my Geiger counter that this water isn't very radioactive,"

▲ Paul taking more sand samples in his backyard beach.
◀ Far left: Paul using a Geiger counter to take radiation measurements of seaweed.

"his house is chock-full of an eclectic collection of microscopes, geiger counters, beakers & sand sifters"

Paul says as he hovers his instrument over a large bucket of freshly collected water. In the heat of the midday sun, we drive to a few different locations gathering water samples. This is common practice for Paul, and as I sit there next to him I'm struck by the fact that Paul may be the only person on the continent doing this type of work.

"We are witnessing a trainwreck, and one thing about trainwrecks is that they're very hard to stop once they've started," he tells me. Coral bleaching has grabbed most of the headlines when it comes to the reef, but Paul has also been monitoring microplastic pollution. Microplastics are wreaking havoc on every marine ecosystem – most alarmingly in areas that aren't responsible for dumping plastic into the ocean.

"This is from Panasesa Island, a tiny uninhabited island hundreds of miles off the coast of Papua New Guinea," Paul says as he shows me a vial full of marble-sized weathered ocean plastic. If plastic can appear in the unpopulated corners of the South Pacific, then it can certainly be found on the beaches of Northern Australia.

▼ A green turtle on Ribbon Reef.
▶ Paul taking a walk along the sand
flats at low tide with his dog, Tombi.

Paul has been working closely with Stuart Mills, Curator of Geoscience at Victoria Museum, on the 'Microplastic contamination in the northern Great Barrier Reef' project. It's goal is to taxonomize the types and sizes of plastics found in Australia's oceans and beaches.

To do this properly, Paul has developed a DIY science lab right in his backyard. Using PVC pipes, coffee filters and a tremendous amount of creativity, he's gathered beach sand from North Queensland and Papua New Guinea with the goal of documenting the concentration of plastics.

EXPLORING THE REEF

You don't have to travel far to find plastic. We take a short boat ride out to Low Isles, a densely forested pair of islands a few miles off the coast. These small islands are usually heavily visited by tourists, but during the pandemic, Paul and I are the only people there. With a sand sifter in his hand and a child-like enthusiasm, he wades into the water and starts collecting samples from the shoreline. As the water cascades out of the bottom of his pan,

I can't help but wonder what sort of contaminants are hidden in that sand.

To mark the end of our trip, we dive below the surface and experience the natural beauty of the reef, spotting the green turtles, black tip reef sharks and coral that make this place a must-see. Undoubtedly, the reef's best days are behind it, but moments of breathtaking beauty aren't in short supply. And with people like Paul around to educate the next generation of caretakers, let's hope there'll be many more of these moments for years to come.

Just before I pull out of his driveway for the 34-hour road trip back to Sydney, I ask Paul what success looks like for him. He looks me right in the eyes and says: "Success can be defined by ambition, but I'm not ambitious. It can be economic goals, but I have no metrics for that. Success for me would be a total cultural paradigm shift where everyone knows how nature is connected and it's no longer an academic pursuit." This paradigm shift is certainly under way, and Paul continues to swim against the currents of environmental destruction. ●

"success for me would be a total cultural paradigm shift where everyone knows how nature is connected and it's no longer an academic pursuit"

everyday adventures

Millican is founded on the idea that we want a better alternative for the bag on your back. We make bags and accessories for a life of mindful adventure.

Based on a farm in the Lake District National Park, Millican was established 12 years ago by Jorrit and Nicky, and is named after the self-confessed 'Professor of Adventure' Millican Dalton – a local Lake District legend who lived out most of his life in a cave in Borrowdale Valley in the early 1900s. He was a maverick of his time.

Our bags are inspired by our natural surroundings and outside living, using recycled and organic materials, led by a simple philosophy 'Use Less, Be More'. Our products are designed to take you anywhere, while striving towards having the least impact possible on the planet – treading lightly as we go. When the world moves fast, we strive to be slow.

 @homeofmillican

homeofmillican.com

Smith the Roll Pack 25L
Simple and lightweight, allowing you to travel further for longer. Ideal for the mountain trail or city commute, with discreet pockets for your essentials.

Fraser the Rucksack 25L
Inspired by alpine explorers, we combined rugged reliability with modern functionality to create a durable bag for all seasons.

Fraser the Rucksack 32L
Like the bags favoured by past alpine explorers, we've kept Fraser lightweight and added modern details, such as hidden pockets.

Nick the Messenger Bag
One of the most practical shoulder bags around, we've added modern details such as a laptop compartment and external water bottle pocket.

Tinsley the Tote Pack 14L
Ideal as a lightweight tote bag for around town, the multifunctional handles convert to make a backpack with adjustable shoulder straps.

Miles the Duffle Bag 40L
Inspired by the usability and simplicity of the legendary duffle bag, we added subtle details to create a workhorse for modern life.

The Core Roll Pack 20L
Functional for daily use, carrying what you need to get from A to B without fuss or compromise on aesthetics, rain or shine.

The Core Roll Pack 15L
A water bottle holder, internal pockets and key loop means you're set for your day wherever you go. Made from post-consumer plastic waste.

Smith the Roll Pack 18L
Geared up for daily use, it's light, tough and sustainable, with a hidden laptop sleeve and internal pockets that make life easier on the road.

TRAIN DREAMS

In the age of *flygskam* (noun, Swedish: the feeling of climate guilt associated with airline travel, literally 'flight shame'), even more of us are looking for an alternative – helping the environment and investing in our own comfort and the idea of journey. **Dan Richards** recounts his nocturnal adventures and the recent renaissance in European sleeper trains.

WORDS: **DAN RICHARDS**
ILLUSTRATIONS: **SAM BREWSTER**

The view from the cab is a galaxy of stars – fluorescent yellows, reds and greens, the dazzling lights of other trains – floating in space; approaching dreamlike before closing to strobe and howl. Raindrops bounce off the windscreen. The wipers swish, we zoom into night. And always the silver rails spooling; a clear road ahead snaking deep into the dark.

A vision from last night's train trip, the 23:45 Lowlander heading north from London Euston to Edinburgh. A new train with automatic doors and locking cabins, it looked, as a fellow passenger noted, "Snazzy."

Several years ago I caught a rather more dowdy sleeper from Euston up to Rannoch Moor for the start of a long hike across the Cairngorms. That journey was somewhat harrowing – nothing to do with the elderly rolling stock; a lack of locks were the least of my troubles. Alas, I'd become a tad inebriated with a friend in the restaurant car while studying the maps for our impending walk. By the time we got to Preston we were good friends with the guard and crew – all doubtless well practiced in humouring those who'd taken the sleeper's late licence as an invitation to get squiffy. The result of that merry evening was a problematic night. I was in the top bunk of our small cabin and have vivid memories of… feeling rather unwell.

Next morning, I awoke so hungover that I regretted surviving the night. I spent the next week stumbling up mountains and down into bogs in thunderstorms, haar and baking heat, which probably served me right.

I certainly don't blame the train.

Night trains have always been synonymous with mystery and possibility for me. The idea of going to sleep in one place and waking in another is a magical 'while you were sleeping we pulled the rug, moved the scenery, sped you somewhere new' sleight of hand. Added to which, nine times out of 10, one actually gets a good night's rest rather than the cramped and crumpled

"How civilised to drift off, swaddled in a sleeper's soft concertina of train songs. To fall asleep imagining the driver's eye view"

half-sleep you get on a bus, with a rolled-up coat as a pillow. Who wouldn't swap that in a blink for real sleep in a bed with sheets and a duvet? How civilised to drift off, swaddled in a sleeper's soft concertina of train songs. To fall asleep imagining the driver's eye view, those infinite arrows of rails and light.

The UK currently has two sleeper services; the GWR Night Riviera, which runs from London Paddington to Cornwall, and The Caledonian Sleeper, which speeds from Euston to various parts of Scotland, but as recently at the early 1990s a nocturnal network ushered small hour travellers out from Kings Cross to Newcastle; Paddington to Milford Haven; Euston to Holyhead; Liverpool and Manchester; Nottingham to Glasgow; Plymouth and Bristol up to Birmingham and York. There were international through-sleepers from London to Brussels and Paris.

In 2017, sleepers in general seemed an endangered species as, across Europe, country after country discontinued their services – France, Switzerland and then, finally, Germany in 2016. Yet, only four years later, the market is experiencing a wonderful renaissance and we have Austria's national railway operator, ÖBB, to thank.

A REJUVENATED TRADITION

Earlier this year I sat down in Vienna with Bernhard Reider of ÖBB to ask him about the company's role in saving the European sleeper. "2016 was the turning point," he told me. Even with Europe's long tradition of night trains, when Germany ceased its sleeper operations, it was a tough decision for the company as to whether they stick with their small network of eight lines, or twist and look outwards; reinvest and refocus on the sleeper market. "And when the decision was made in 2016, it wasn't clear that it would be successful." But the past three years have proven them right, especially 2019, which saw a dramatic change in demand.

"Before now we saw that trains were busy in the holidays – Christmas, Easter, and Summer was always full," Bernhard enthused. "We always used to say, 'if you want to travel in November or December on a Tuesday, you will always find spaces' – that's changed completely in the past 15 months. Now, even on those days we are completely full in the sleeping cars. We've found that people are willing to pay for their trip. They're not only looking for the €30 flight from Cologne to Vienna." In the age of *flygskam* (noun, Swedish: the feeling of climate guilt associated with airline travel, literally 'flight shame'), people are thinking before buying a plane ticket, looking for an alternative, specifically looking to take the train. "This is the big change: that people are willing to invest for the environment, the comfort, the idea of journey."

Looking back, one of the most exciting and heartening parts of our conversation was the fact that Bernhard spoke of 'the Greta Thunberg effect' without a hint of cynicism.

Having started with eight lines, ÖBB now runs 27 together with its international partners. "I think it's quite a good number!" Bernhard said, smiling. "We have recently invested more than €200 million in 13 new Nightjet trains, which will be completely different." Some of the current rolling stock has been in service for 30 years – it's worn out. Yes, the snazzy double-decker Doppelstock sleeping cars run in and out of Zurich but they're the exception.

The design of the new trains factors in trends and passenger expectations, the biggest being privacy. At the moment they run a maximum of two sleeping coaches per train but the focus has now shifted to the idea of sleepers as top-end travelling hotels with en suite compartments as standard. At the same time, formerly communal cars of couchettes will be upgraded to compartments of mini-suites of bijou compartment with shuttered walls that passengers can close around themselves, "so it's small but you can sleep in privacy; nobody else will be next to you; and that you can have for quite a low price."

ÖBB's new Nightjets will enter service shortly on lines between Austria and Italy. In 2019 they launched a new route from Berlin to Vienna, and this year sees the introduction of new sleepers between Brussels, Vienna and Munich, as well as the much anticipated service to Amsterdam. Added to which, the Scandinavians are now getting in on the act with STA of Sweden mooting a new route overnight from Malmö to London.

Travelling to Vienna, I had a cabin to myself – which was marvellous and quite rare. Generally there are 'other people' and 'ladders' involved – which is a different sort of fun, an "Oh, hello! You're sleeping here too? How fun! Where are we? Do you need me to shift so you can climb that ladder? Yes, ha, it is quite snug. Pardon? Ah. I'm sorry, my German is very poor… yes, and my French as well…" sort of fun. But, as it was, I could settle down at once, get cosy, turn the lights off, open the blinds and watch the winter night spool past – sheer mountains in the moonlight, cosy villages glimpsed in a whirl of snow, mighty rivers far below precipitous viaducts, deep dark forests and, always, the warmth of knowing that I was off on a great adventure while in bed.

AN ALL MOD CONS POD

One of the great things about bijou sleeper travel is that almost everything is within arm's reach from one's bunk. There are handy pockets for water bottles and buttons and dials for reading lights and air-con – all of which will be explained by your steward on arrival. Then, after you've filled in the standard tick box selection for next morning's breakfast, they'll usually give you a key card to lock your door and wish you a good night. You're then at liberty to pad up and down the carriage to the shower and washroom as much as you like, explore the train – wish all the poor bastards in the seated compartments an over-cheery "Good evening!" (unless you're only going a short distance, sleeper seats are rotten and a contradiction in terms), and see if the train has a bar… after which one can turn-in to one's cot and write postcards on one's knees – "Caught sleeper train all right. Am in bed! Everyone speaks wonderful English. Yet again, my lack of language skills make me feel like a terrible dolt. Will have to learn fluent German as soon as I get home…"

That coach was a mix of families and couples, mostly journeying tourists. I'd spotted a few business people on the platform at Cologne – long-padded jackets over suits; caterpillars with shiny shoes. Sleeper folk were still boarding several hours after I'd gone to bed, lying in the rushing dark, muzzily aware of sliding doors and people excitedly whispering as they made their way past to their

> "I could settle down at once, get cosy, turn the lights off, open the blinds and watch the winter night spool past"

bunks. Somewhere en route carriages were shunted off to join other trains for Munich and Innsbruck and others attached from who knows where.

And perhaps it's worth noting that every one of my sleeper journeys has felt safe. There are actually far fewer murders on sleeper trains than Agatha Christie would have you believe; people are generally friendly and hospitable. So do board your blue train reassured. (Sleeper trains seem to be either green or blue. NightJet trains are electric indigo, often pulled by impressive crimson locomotives. The Caledonian Sleeper runs in 'Midnight Teal' with antler motifs. GWR's Night Riviera is deep Brunswick green.) The whole thing is jolly romantic and exciting. Even 'railway coffee' and a bacon sandwich in a foil-bag become Ambrosian when eaten on a sleeper scooting through the Cornish dawn. ●

raptor persecution

At the height of lockdown, while all the hillwalkers were stuck inside throwing lunges in front of Joe Wicks, something sinister was going on in our deserted countryside. The RSPB reported an unprecedented surge in "orchestrated" illegal bird of prey killings, as perpetrators took advantage of a temporary lack of witnesses. Raptor persecution is nothing new. Birds like hen harriers, buzzards and goshawks are trapped, shot or poisoned, usually to stop them preying on more lucrative game birds.

Outdoor Provisions, who make tasty, natural energy bars in flavours themed around national parks, are committed to protecting our beautiful birds of prey. A proportion of their profits goes towards helping the RSPB investigate raptor persecution – so as you head out into the Peak District with a cherry bakewell bar or bite down on a treacly parkin snack in the Yorkshire Dales, you'll be supporting some of the area's most embattled residents. "Birds are key to our experiences of the outdoors," says Christian from Outdoor Provisions. "It links in with ideas of land access and land ownership." And he's keen to stress how urgently we need to act – some species like hen harriers are already teetering on the brink of extinction.

We can all do our bit to protect birds of prey while we're out in the countryside. Keep an eye out for traps or dead raptors, especially if there's a half-finished meal nearby, which could indicate poisoned bait. If you do find anything suspicious, get photos and a GPS location if you can, report it to the police non-emergency number and inform the RSPB. You can also show your support by ordering a £6 raptor pin badge from Outdoor Provisions, of which 100% of the profits will go to supporting the RSPB's investigations into illegal wildlife crime.

OUTDOOR PROVISIONS

working together
giving
nature
a home
with the rspb

1%
FOR THE PLANET.

BUZZARD
Buteo buteo
WINGSPAN 115cm -130cm

GOLDEN EAGLE
Aquila chrysaetos
WINGSPAN 190-225cm

MARSH HARRIER
Circus aeruginosus
WINGSPAN 110-125cm

OSPREY
Pandion haliaetus
WINGSPAN 145-160cm

PEREGRINE FALCON
Falco peregrinus
WINGSPAN 95-115cm

RED KITE
Milvus milvus
WINGSPAN 145-165cm

SPARROWHAWK
Accipiter nisus
WINGSPAN 60-75cm

KESTREL
Falco tinnunculus
WINGSPAN 65-80cm

GOSHAWK
Accipiter gentilis
WINGSPAN 95-120cm

MERLIN
Falco columbarius
WINGSPAN 60-65cm.

HOBBY
Falco subbuteo
WINGSPAN 70-85cm

BRITISH RAPTORS

sea nomads

Armed with sunglasses to protect his eyes from
the dagger-like bills, **Sam Hobson** joins the seabirders,
a group of scientists on the frontline of Britain's
gannet study and conservation effort

WORDS & PHOTOS: **SAM HOBSON**

from outlandish tales of swallows lying torpid for the winter in the crevices of lake beds, to stories of the hoopoe sleeping in winter "like the bat", bird migration has long been a matter of speculation. In recent decades, internationally coordinated studies and bird ringing records have helped shed light on the incredible migratory journeys of many birds, but seabirds have remained particularly elusive. They are creatures of habit when it comes to breeding and can be studied in detail for a few short months at nesting colonies, but often spend most of the year as nomadic seafarers, traversing oceans, obscured by sea-mists and wild weather – out of sight and unfathomable.

However, modern technology is changing this and, for the first time, detailed data is being gathered by intrepid scientists, who venture out to islands around the UK to capture and fit seabirds with GPS loggers and finally discover their secrets. I spent a summer following a team of researchers undertaking a pioneering study into the foraging behaviours of our largest seabird – the northern gannet – which took me to the 'Scottish Alcatraz', camping on the plug of an extinct volcano, and joining a vital rescue mission on a remote Welsh island.

LANDING ON THE BASS

After days of waiting for a window in the weather, we are heading out into the Firth of Forth on the east coast of Scotland. The swell suddenly builds as we approach The Bass Rock, and as the boat pitches and throws us all off balance, we experience a full-on attack to the senses.

Already disoriented and struggling to gather my gear together, I'm deafened by the clangour of the largest colony of northern gannets in the world – 150,000 strong. That's when the ammonia smell of guano hits and takes my breath away. Suddenly I feel small and entirely out of my element. Landing on The Bass is like stepping into Conan Doyle's *The Lost World*, where prehistoric creatures roam. Gannets are Britain's largest and most formidable seabird, and now I'm face-to-face with one, this becomes immediately apparent.

It's gannet breeding season and I'm accompanying researchers from Leeds University – James Grecian, Jude Lane, Helen Wade and Keith Hamer – who are hoping to recapture adult gannets fitted with data-loggers as they return to their nests from long foraging trips. Exactly where these birds have been is what they're trying to find out, as proposed offshore wind farms have the potential to seriously disrupt the feeding patterns of the colony.

We start the trek up into the heart of the colony, located at the ruined chapel of St Baldred – a sixth-century monk, who lived as a hermit on The Bass. James leads the way, but it isn't long before he is forced to down tools and confront a couple of burly looking jailbirds blocking the path. They have taken up residence in the old prison, apparently known as the 'Scottish Alcatraz', where religious and political prisoners were locked up in the 17th century. We clear a path so they have an escape route, and James opens the gate and flushes them out without hesitation. He has done this before.

I'm apprehensive as we exit the safety of the prison walls as, 10 years previously, on another visit, this stretch was the haunt of nesting herring and great black-backed gulls, and I not only got peppered with gull droppings, but my sun hat was stolen by a particularly aggressive gull, who I'm sure I heard laughing as he carried it out to sea.

"landing on
the bass is like
stepping into
conan doyle's
the lost world"

This time, however, there's no room for gulls.
The gannets are everywhere and there's barely room
to step through them. Now I can see now why everyone
is wearing glasses as the gannets stab at each other and
us with six-inch-long, dagger-like bills.

The team sets up a base when we arrive at the chapel,
and it's the first time I can stop and take in the spectacle
of the place. I can see why the island looks so white from
the mainland as the sun bounces off the birds and layers
of guano. It reminds me of a passage in *Moby Dick*, when
Melville describes the whiteness of the whale: "And yet
this mere aspect of all-pervading whiteness makes him
more strangely hideous than the ugliest abortion."

What you don't see from the mainland is the amount
of activity. It's hard to take in any single event in this
heaving metropolis, with birds constantly coming,
going and circling overhead, like "phantoms rising in
a milk-white fog" as Melville might describe them.

It's quickly back to business though, as adult birds are
singled out to recapture and immature birds are selected
to attach with high-resolution GPS loggers for the first
time. These will help the team track the birds' flights in
3D, so they can determine the average altitude at which
they fly when foraging and whether that might conflict
with the rotor-blades of the proposed turbines.

Watching the team in action as they capture and
tag the gannets is an eye-opening experience.
They are typical 'seabirders': quite unassuming on the
surface, but with an obvious deep passion for the sea,
islands and more often than not, big, burly birds,
which they seem to unflinchingly grapple with in the
name of science. Despite all of this, there isn't a hint
of machismo and as is the case with this team, women
and men are quite evenly represented. In the otherwise
male-dominated world of birding, seabirders are about
as far as you can get from the the typical image of
the solitary twitcher, sitting in a bird-hide with his
sandwiches, ticking off little-brown-jobs.

It now becomes apparent what the long, cumbersome rods we've carried up here are for. I watch a researcher extend one out into the throng of birds and delicately place a small noose around a gannet's neck. He now has what is essentially a powerful, angry bird on the end of a stick. He wrestles it into submission so that it can be weighed and fitted with a GPS device and Darvic leg ring for future identification. It often takes two or more people to process each bird and I'm glad I'm not one of them.

CAMPING ON AILSA CRAIG

A few weeks later I travel with the team to the next stop on the other side of the country, Ailsa Craig. Just off the west coast of Scotland in the Firth of Clyde, it is the granite plug of an extinct volcano. The granite has such low water absorption, that for a long time, it was the only quarry from which Olympic curling stones were made. On arrival, it's hard to imagine that 70,000 gannets inhabit the colony as they're tucked away on a sheer cliff on the far side of the island. We're greeted by a man named Bernie, whose lined face, weathered by sun and salt, gives me a sense of what it might mean to be a lifelong seabirder.

Unlike on Bass, we can stay on Ailsa, so once tents are pitched, we head up to the summit. The way is littered with bird carcasses, mainly puffins and guillemots caught and picked apart by the gulls. At the top, we pause to see if we can get a signal to track the tagged birds, but it's too weak, so we carefully pick our way down through the puffin burrows to the cliff edge. There James and Jude find a good signal so they can download data remotely. It's now just a waiting game for the logged birds to return from foraging trips, which can be two days long, and can take them to the coasts of Norway. Despite the wait, James remains focused and is visibly excited every time a bird comes close enough to download its data: "It's been impossible to know exactly where these birds forage until now. This is the first time we will have the high resolution

data needed to discover how they find food," he tells me.

Camping on a seabird island is an otherworldly experience, often accompanied by the eerie wails of nocturnal seabirds and spectral glimpses of wraithlike shapes flying through the gloom, but Ailsa completes the experience with its mysterious, unearthly terrain. Exploring at twilight, we find ourselves circumambulating the island on a sketchy wooden walkway, crumbling and wave-battered, like something out of an Indiana Jones film. As darkness descends further, we come upon a giant foghorn, sinister in size and appearance, redolent of stormy nights and sunken ships.

In the morning, I get to chat to Bernie and listen to some of his stories. On and off Ailsa for nearly 40 years, he led the rat extermination effort in the early 90s and by 2002, thanks to his efforts, the puffins were back. Sharing a cup of tea outside his hut, he explains his method of luring storm petrels into large nets at night by blasting recordings of their calls out to sea.

We head up to the colony to see if any further tagged birds have returned, and after a long day, the fieldwork is over. Months of work collating, analysing and making sense of the data now lie ahead.

Just as we reach the ruined castle on our way down to meet the boat, we're treated to a wildlife spectacle like nothing I've seen. Just offshore, hundreds of gannets are gathering, and from our elevated position I can appreciate just how high they're preparing to dive from. The first one dives and quickly, they all start dropping. It's hard to believe any of them will survive, plummeting 50 metres and smashing face-first into the sea. The smack of the surface breaking as bird after bird hits is palpable, and as they plunge after fish, the trail of bubbles left in the water reveals just how deep they dive. It's suddenly clear why only 30 per cent of gannets make it to adulthood. We watch speechless for 10 minutes until the frenzy dissipates. I gladly realise I didn't diminish the experience by reaching for my camera. We head back to the

"the seaweed perishes & disappears, leaving 20 tonnes of plastic"

◀ Tim among the gannet nests on Grassholm, which is beginning to resemble a landfill site.
▼ Hanging from a cliff with a noose around its neck, this bird was one of the lucky few to be rescued.

mainland, wave goodbye to Bernie at the fish and chip shop and I begin my journey south.

A RESCUE MISSION ON GRASSHOLM

I'm due to join a rescue mission that only happens once a year when conditions allow. I catch the boat at St Justinian's, Pembrokeshire, and we head out to pick up Greg and Lisa Morgan, wardens of RSPB Ramsey Island, who are leading the mission. We're heading to Grassholm Island, eight miles off the mainland and home to 39,000 pairs of northern gannets – 10 per cent of the world's population. Its location brings the birds into contact with Atlantic currents that carry material from as far away as the east coast of the United States and northwest Africa.

Traditionally, gannets made use of this by collecting floating seaweed to line their nests, but that weed is now entangled with fishing nets, packing straps, balloons and other plastic fibres. At the end of the season, when the island is deserted, the weed perishes and disappears, leaving just the waste material, which has built up into 20 tonnes of plastic. These strong, man-made fibres are a death trap. Entangled adults have a fighting chance, but weaker juveniles often become knotted in their plastic nests – constricted and deformed as they grow.

There's no messing about when we land, and the team is off. There's a sense of urgency and it's hard to keep up. As the volunteers spread out, most birds take flight, leaving only those physically tethered to the island. I follow Greg and my heart is in my mouth as he creeps to the edge of a cliff, risking his life to grab hold of a panicked adult dangling from a cliff with a noose around its neck.

I look around and it's like a rubbish tip. I notice a severed gannet's foot, tangled in twine and picture the desperate struggle that left it behind. Skipper Tim Brooke remembers his first visit to Grassholm 25 years ago before marine litter was a problem: "People used to look after their lines and fix their nets, but now it's cheaper just to chuck them."

In just a few hours, the team has cut 50 birds free and the whole thing is finished just as quickly as it started. As I make my way back to the boat, struggling to keep up with the others, I stumble across a juvenile, alone in its plastic nest. It reminds me of an 'endling' - the last of a species before extinction. I look around desperately for someone to help, but it's down to me. I don the my sunglasses and get out my pen knife. Adrenaline pumping, I go for it and after a short tussle, somehow manage not to make a hash of it. Shaky, I leave the liberated nestling, knowing it might not survive, but it feels right to give it a chance.

On the boat, I ask Greg why they can't just remove the plastic: "These birds return to the same nests every year and removing them would be too disruptive to the colony. All we can do is firefight the problem," he says.

Compared to mainland Europe, Britain has lost much of its most impressive wildlife, but it punches well above its weight when it comes to seabirds. Spending time with the researchers gives me the sense that seabirds act as a canary in the coal-mine with regards to the health of our oceans. As James says: "It's our duty to understand changes in the marine environment and how they have been brought on by the Anthropocene." With two-thirds of the world's population of northern gannets found in the UK, he's right. Our behaviour directly affects the entire global species. I've barely scratched the surface of this story, but I'm left hopeful that people like James and the other seabirders are out there on the frontline. If nothing else, I have definitely caught the seabirding bug. ●

Out of the corner of your eye you spot some movement in a hedgerow, it's a tiny Wren busily hopping from one branch to another, such a small bird, so much energy.

While walking through a wooded river valley you turn the corner to find a rocky ravine absolutely covered in thick moss. Crouching down to see how the moss looks like a forest in miniature and find delight in losing yourself in a minuscule world.

Magic.

Finding a big old oak to sit under, watching tadpoles in a pond, finding the perfect blackberry, the colours of autumn, watching the sea mist roll in over the land, the list goes on and on!

Yes, that's right, outside lies magic.
It can be found in the big, but equally in the small.

Like you, we have a love of the outdoors. Being a rural design studio, nature is a source of endless inspiration. We also frickin love stationery. Notebooks in particular. So we thought why not combine both these passions and create a little ode to the outdoors.

This is the result, a hardy yet beautiful set of A6 recycled notebooks. We went to town obsessing over the details simply because, that's what we do.

If we were going to release a set of notebooks, we wanted the best recycled papers. The covers are a thick (380gsm) paper that's made from upcycled coffee cups and, with use, ages like a great pair of jeans (we know, we field tested them ourselves). The inner pages are a smooth 100% recycled plain paper which is a joy to write on.

We couldn't resist, for that extra bit of magic we used an iridescent gold foil (it changes colour at different angles!) to show off the beautiful hand lettered cover design. The icing on the cake!

We're super proud of these.
We know you'll love them too.

Available online at: studiointhesticks.com/magic

Studio in the Sticks is a design studio, nestled upon a hill on Dartmoor. We work with folk like you, the brave, visionary, imaginative ones out there on a mission to change things for the better.

website: studiointhesticks.com/magic
newsletter: studiointhesticks.com/for-the-curious
instagram: @studiointhesticks

THE ROOT BRIDGES OF MEGHALAYA

Grown over decades from the roots of the rubber fig tree, the bridges of Meghalaya are testament to a living architecture that crosses time and ancestry, as well as the gushing gorges of the Khasi hills

WORDS & PHOTOS: **WILLEM BETTS**

a *ryngkew*, a shapeshifting and occasionally malevolent forest spirit that local people are careful not to disturb. Jallong finishes his meal and begins packing his homemade wooden pipe with dark, stringy tobacco. I ask if the *ryngkew* can still be heard.

"No, he doesn't speak anymore. Disappeared. When the villagers left, he also left." He exhales a cloud of smoke from his nostrils and looks in the direction of the river. "But I think he's still there. With a giant, ancient tree like that, why would he leave? That kind of creature would stick around."

LAND OF WATER

Aside from a few outliers, living root bridges can only be found in the Riwar, a rugged region where the highlands of Meghalaya fall away suddenly to the plains of northern Bangladesh. It's a landscape of extremes, with densely forested valleys so steep you can barely find a place to lie down. There are almost no roads, so locals like Jallong rely on a network of footpaths to access their plantations and bring their goods to market. It also happens to be one of the rainiest places on Earth – the weather station in the nearby town of Sohra once measured 9.3 metres of rain in a single month, 16 times what London receives in a year. When this volume of water enters the valleys of the Riwar, trickling streams become raging, dangerous torrents.

Where these rivers need to be crossed, locals plant *ficus elastica*, a species of rubber fig related to the banyan tree that produces prodigious amounts of flexible aerial roots from its upper branches. These roots, fast-growing and aggressively attaching wherever they're tied, are the perfect

J allong Khongmawloh has never worn shoes in his life. His feet are muscular, the skin on his sole a smooth, thick pad, built up from decades of walking through the forest. I've come to his bamboo hut, in a grove of orange trees in the far north-east corner of India, to ask him about the bridge that crosses the nearby Risam river. Jallong is an elder of the Khasi tribe, one of three tribes from the state of Meghalaya. He unfolds a dried leaf of areca palm and reveals his lunch: some kind of large, bitter orange, fried in oil with turmeric, served on a bed of white rice. He eats with his hands.

"Back when there was a village in this forest, people were afraid to walk on the bridge," he tells me. "They were afraid because when they did, a voice would call out, shouting 'Hey! Don't step on me!'"

The Risam bridge is a *Jingkieng jri*, a bridge made from the living roots of a rubber fig tree. Its growth was guided across the river decades ago, using traditional methods perfected over the centuries by members of the Khasi and Jaintia tribes. At some point, the bridge became home to

"These roots, fast-growing and aggressively attaching wherever they're tied, are the perfect material for building living bridges"

◀ Although this immature bridge is useable, it will take at least a decade to widen the deck and add railings.

material for building living bridges. A root no thicker than a shoelace can grow strong enough to carry a person's weight after five years. It could take 30 to 50 years for a bridge to become mature, with local oral history placing the oldest bridges in Meghalaya at around 500 years old.

Jallong uses his pocket knife to remove the dense orange husk from a betel nut and offers me a piece. I politely decline – last time I tried one my whole body flushed red and I was too dizzy to walk. Instead he passes it to my interpreter, Morningstar Khongthaw.

"A root no thicker than a shoelace can grow strong enough to carry a person's weight after five years"

Morningstar is a 23-year-old guide and environmental activist from Rangthylliang. He was a teenager when an American explorer, Patrick Rogers, visited the village looking for root bridges to document in his travel book *The Green Unknown* (2017). Morningstar accompanied Patrick through the forest, showing him many of the bridges his family had been using for generations. With Patrick's encouragement, Morningstar decided that instead of attending college, he would build a tourism business in his home village, a place that happened to have a high concentration of root bridges. He and some local villagers established a tourism society, and after receiving a land grant from the village council, they pooled their money together and established a roadside viewpoint. Nobody came, and after a few monsoon seasons the bamboo buildings rotted and collapsed.

It would be two years before Morningstar would have his first client, but in the meantime, he explored. He travelled throughout the Riwar, to places that had never seen a tourist, and built relationships with local farmers, village headmen, distant relatives, and anyone

◀ Far left: This bridge began as a single root that was fixed across the massive ravine in 1968.

Concerned that the root bridge tradition was in decline, Morningstar became an activist. With the help of his friends, he established the Living Bridge Foundation, the first organization dedicated to root bridge conservation. Its members are a group of dedicated root bridge exponents from throughout Meghalaya who come together to share knowledge and encourage villages to maintain and multiply their local bridges.

FOES TO FRIENDS

It's late afternoon, and time to go home. Morningstar and I wait while Jallong packs his conical basket full of *lakor*, the waxy leaf chewed along with betel nut. He hoists it on to his back, the weight beared by a woven plastic strap across his forehead, and we begin our hike into the forest, where we immediately find ourselves beneath the awesome canopy of the *Risam ficus*. Dim shafts of crepuscular light stream through the branches and illuminate the tree's massive trunk. Recently, Jallong and other elders from Rangthylliang planned to chop this tree down, including the bridge, and turn it all into charcoal. Jallong's concern was that the tree, showing no sign of slowing growth in spite of its advanced age, was starting to shade his clearing, stealing sunlight from his orange trees. As soon as he heard of this plan, Morningstar approached the owner of the tree (in the Khasi hills you can own a tree without owning the land it sits on) and convinced him to sell it to him for the price of the charcoal they would earn from it.

Their dispute over the Risam tree put Morningstar and Jallong at odds with one another, but the two are good friends now, and I observe nothing but mutual respect between them. As we step on to the interwoven roots of the bridge, Jallong says to Morningstar, "You'll be remembered for saving this tree. It will live on for the next generation. When people take care of the tree, the Ryngkew lives here happily. He won't get angry; he won't attack you." We continue across the bridge, hearing nothing but the sound of birds. ●

Learn more about the Living Bridge Foundation at **facebook.com/morningstarfounder**

who might lead a tour group should any finally come. With his new friends' help, Morningstar located dozens of bridges previously unknown to the outside world.

However, Morningstar found that not all of his fellow Khasi were as enthusiastic about their root bridge heritage as he was. New roads were being built and old foot trails abandoned. Ancient bridges had become neglected, their once carefully maintained forms overgrown into a chaotic mess. When root bridges died, Morningstar saw that villagers were eschewing the years-long process of establishing new ones, opting instead for steel suspension bridges. These can be built faster, last a long time, and the cost of labour and materials are often paid for by the Indian government through village development schemes. I ask Morningstar why this troubles him: "No root bridge can be built by one person alone; when we tie a fresh root on to an old bridge, we're collaborating with our ancestors as well as our descendants. When we lose one, a connection to our culture is severed."

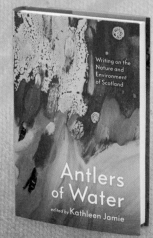

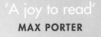

subscribe

Treat yourself to a subscription and you'll receive 10% off. It's an ideal gift for completists who love to see their journals stacking up neatly on their bookshelves as much as we do.

Ernest Journal is published every six to nine months. You can start your subscription from either the current or upcoming edition.

A one-year subscription comprises two issues and costs £18, plus p&p. A two-year subscription comprises four issues and comes to £36, plus p&p.

Subscriptions and pre-orders are essential for sustaining the journal – so a huge thank you to everyone who supports our indie publishing project in this way!

Islands

The lofotfiske | History of the Rorbu | The surfers of Unstad

RUSSIA

RUS

Shetland birds | The Good Shepherd | The knitters of Fair Isle

Laurisilva | Levada walks | Monte Toboggan Run

Islands provoke a feeling of being on the edge – of the ocean, or the world, or even the limits of human life. Just getting there can be an adventure, whether we're skimming cliffs to land on a short runway, or bumping across the North Sea in a steel-hulled freighter. Extremes of weather and geography force us to travel slowly, and a strip of land a few miles long can contain thousands of years of history and culture.

In a year where we've all experienced isolation, islands take this to the extreme, and the curious thing about seclusion from the outside world is that it provides ideal conditions for both evolution and preservation. Some things evolve in unique ways, like the daredevil toboggans of Funchal or the *lofotfiske* fishing season on Lofoten, while other things that were once widespread now survive only in these remote environments – like the subtropical laurel forest of Madeira, which once blanketed much of southern Europe.

As we explore Fair Isle, Madeira and the Lofoten Islands, we find surprising places where ingenuity and adaptation are at a premium, and where communities are even tighter for their isolated lives out there on the edge.

ILLUSTRATIONS: **AIDAN MEIGHAN**

island of eternal spring

Sub-tropical laurisilva | Levada walks |
Ponta do Pargo Lighthouse |
The Monte Toboggan Run

WORDS & PHOTOS: **DAN COOK**

As our plane circles over the endless blue of the Atlantic, Madeira emerges sharply above the water. If wishing to picture the topography of the archipelago, you might turn to Robert White and James Yate Johnson's 1860 book *Madeira: Its Climate and Scenery*. Take a sheet of paper, it suggests, crush it in your hand then partly open it out and place it on the table with the highest point directed to the ceiling.

A CLOSE APPROACH

We are destined for Madeira, the largest island of the group, lured by the promise of sub-tropical climate, knife-edge mountain walks, rare plant life and giant sea cliffs. Yet today's tourist-driven economy conceals the challenges that have faced Madeirans in sustaining life here, 300 miles from the west coast of Africa, perched on the slopes of an ancient volcano.

Our first challenge is landing safely on an island where level ground makes up less than 10 per cent of its surface. While the captain navigates one of the most dangerous runways in Europe, we sit back and watch the jagged cliffs come almost within touching distance.

Our first stop is Funchal, the island's capital on the south coast. Funchal has been the largest settlement since the Portuguese colonised these then-uninhabited islands in 1420. The large, naturally protected bay made it an *entrepôt* for centuries of seafaring traders from Europe, driven here by the trade winds. The islanders prospered from a convenient position on the trade routes, but being at the mercy of distant wars, politics and technology has often caused the prosperity of Madeira to fluctuate, much like the landscape on which its residents reside.

Today, Madeira draws in tourists rather than traders. Its most famous export no longer being the Madeira wine of island origin, but island-born Cristiano Ronaldo, whose name adorns the airport.

The next day, beneath an unrelenting sun, we linger on the summit of Pico Ruivo, strong gusts of wind providing welcome relief from the heat of the ascent. Around us, the landscape falls away in a chaos of precipices, pinnacles and gorges.

Here at the highest point of the island (1,862 metres), Madeira's volcanic origins are evident in the turmoil of the textures around us. Pinnacles of dark basalt stand isolated before cliffs layered with the yellows and reds of tufa; stacked layers of rock and ash slant at all angles before dropping away into an abyss. Occasionally horizontal layers are broken by the dark vertical lines of the dykes that once fed this ancient lava to the surface.

Our climb to the summit had begun at the nearby Pico de Arieiro, only 44 metres below us, but nearly three hours of enthralling hiking along an improbable puzzle of tunnels and exposed paths. The route PR1 ('PR'

> "stacked layers of rock and ash slant at all angles before dropping away into an abyss"

standing for *pequeño recorrido* or 'short tour') is an official trail and a prime example of how even the highest and most inaccessible terrain on the island is tamed. Complete with a gift shop, restaurant and car park, the walk tempts many of Madeira's visitors away from their cruise ships and into the interior.

Leaving Pico Ruivo behind, we make our return on foot. Fortunately, many of the groups sharing the summit with us head for their buses instead, leaving us to enjoy a more leisurely return dawdling in the cool tunnels that carve from one side of the island to the other through its highest ridge.

WALKING ON WATER

One resource that Madeira has in plentiful supply is rainwater, which regularly falls on the northern slopes, nourishing the sub-tropical *laurisilva* (laurel forest), before filtering down to layers of volcanic ash below the surface. Springs then form where the water meets impervious rock and form rivers in deep ravines. The water

◀ Previous: View from São Vicente.
▶ Top: Hikers on the PR1 route.
▶ Below: Final ascent to Pico Ruivo.

A LIQUID HISTORY

"Madeira wine is… like drinking liquid history," declared Winston Churchill after sampling a bottle of 1792 Sercial during one of his visits to Madeira in the 1950s. Madeira wine has always travelled well, both in distance and time, and is one of few wines that can be aged over decades, even centuries.

The unique method for producing the Madeira wine we know today was discovered inadvertently some time during the 16th century. After barrels of wine had endured the undulating movements and tropical heat on their voyages to the East Indies, the flavour of the wine was found to have improved. A system for heating the wine over a period of three months, known as estufagem, was devised to replicate this happy accident on land.

▲ Above: Deep in the laurisilva
◀ Left: A levada weaves around the mountains at Encumeada.

pays no attention to the desires of the island inhabitants and heads straight for the sea before plunging into the ocean straight from sheer cliffs.

The *levadas*, which are unique to Madeira, were the colonists' solution to transporting the water before it escaped to the sea. Constructed in the 15th century by contractors who often used convict labour or enslaved Africans, these narrow drainage channels provided drinking water and irrigation away from the ravines and towards the towns and farmlands of the island, where water was scarce.

Today, over 2000km of *levadas* weave around the island, rough-hewn into the relatively soft volcanic rock or transported in simple wooden gutters over harder basalt. In most villages and towns you will find them gently flowing by streets and between houses. Yet the slow, orderly movement of the water in the channels contrasts the challenge of their construction. Many lives were lost as they struggled to break away rock while suspended by ropes above the mountainous terrain.

Now mostly upgraded, the modern *levadas* are of concrete construction. In addition to water, they now carry a mass of hikers who balance along their open edges to penetrate the island's otherwise inaccessible cloud forests.

Our first *levada* experience is PR16 – Levada Fajã do Rodrigues on the north of the island. The guidebook promises an "adventurous tunnel tour through evergreen laurel tropical

"the gentle sounds of the water gliding along the levada has a calming effect"

forest". At the start of the *levada*, a passing local begins a conversation. Unfortunately, due to my very limited Portuguese and my concentration directed more to the sharp edge of the scythe he's gesturing with, we're left unsure if we're being offered advice, a warning or just polite conversation.

We set off heedlessly and soon the rich green density of the ancient *laurisilva* surrounds us. The gentle sounds of the water gliding along the *levada* by our side has a calming effect. A Madeiran chaffinch occasionally joins us in the shade, before darting above the water in search of insects. Madeiran wall lizards scurry away from the shadows warning of our approach. Trout (introduced to the channels each year) race through the water, investigating any potential food that breaks the surface of the clear waters.

Before long, a dark, oval shape greets us as we reach the entrance to our first *levada* tunnel. Our guidebook suggests this is the "nastiest tunnel on the island" and the animal skull hung over the entrance suggests others

▶ Right: Encounter with a bold Madeiran chaffinch.
▶ Right page: Japanese cypress along the PR16 levada.

THE MONTE TOBOGGAN RUN

In the 19th century a new form of transport emerged on the steep, narrow streets of the island's capital Funchal. In the suburbs of Monte, some 600m above downtown Funchal, residents decided to use gravity to solve the problem of transporting people and goods to the city. Wicker toboggans were built and mounted on to greased wooden slats, and the first Carreiros do Monte began to drive the contraptions at speeds of up to 38km/h through the streets.

From their practical beginnings, and despite the modern addition of motorised traffic sharing the roads, the toboggans have become one of the most popular tourist attractions on the island. The Carreiros still adorn the traditional attire of a white shirt, white trousers and a straw hat, while relying on their specialised rubber-soled shoes to steer the toboggans.

thought the same. Sure enough, this is not the careful construction of an Alpine engineered walking route. The rock has been carved out just enough to accommodate the width of the *levada* with a ledge barely wide enough for two feet. Carefully we sidestep through the darkness, occasionally nudged by a protruding mound of rock as it bruises our shoulders. The bumps and grazes seem worth it as we emerge deeper in the *laurisilva*, where a tropical waterfall flows into a pool behind us.

The guidebook recommends returning at this point, but ahead lies another tunnel over 1km long. Tempted by the promise of more

"the easiest or perhaps cheapest option was to wedge the roads precariously on the edge of sea cliffs"

adventures, we spend 10 minutes edging our way into the uncomfortable darkness where our torches now seem useless. The light at the end of the tunnel is a tiny spec, which, despite our approaching steps, never seems to get any closer. Deciding not to go any further, we turn and retreat.

DRIVING ON MOUNTAIN TOPS

Leaving the tunnels behind, we decide to explore more of the island from the comfort of the car. The roads on the island are no less dramatic than the *levadas*, as they cling in snaking patterns to the unstable turmoil of the island's topography. There are plenty of examples of abandoned roads, particularly on the coastal routes. Before the construction of EU-funded tunnels, the easiest or perhaps cheapest option was to wedge the roads precariously on the edge of sea cliffs. We stop to look at one such abandoned road, perched above the crashing waves, eroded and green underneath a tall waterfall that seems to look down and mock the idea that a road existed here.

◀ Left: Mountain roads at Encumeada.
▼ Below: Bridal Veil Falls above an abandoned road on the north coast.

High in the mountains, we reach road signs that indicate dangerous rockfalls ahead. Only a few minutes from our accommodation, we drive on – our second heedless act of the day. Our journey is soon halted not by danger but awe at the sight of a hairpin bend, impossibly perched on the edge of a ridge with vertical drops on all three sides of us. Moving on cautiously, each curve takes us down in altitude as the rock faces grow higher above. Carefully we proceed, passing scatters of rockfall that narrow the road – the volcanic geology continues to claim small victories over the flat asphalt attempting to tame it.

THE EDGE OF THE WORLD
In need of a break from the harsh edges of Madeira's eastern half, the following day we head to the very western tip, Ponta do Pargo (Tip of the Snapper). The early morning brings sounds of farmland originating from somewhere within the thick mist that has settled around us. A westerly blowing in from the Atlantic brings persistent rain, so we spend the time exploring the garden of our accommodation, where succulents thrive in the moist air.

In the afternoon, flashes of blue appear on the horizon as the cloud finally clears. Following *levadas* through the fields, we soon leave behind the white walls of the town and arrive at the Ponta Do Pargo Lighthouse, standing nearly 300 metres above waves clawing at the cliffs below. The tower has been warning of the treacherous waters here for over 100 years; its light capable of reaching out some 26 miles into the Atlantic, where no land rises between here and the Americas.

The cliffs soon come alive with an orange glow and we catch glimpses of what the islanders consider one of the best sunsets in the world. Unfortunately, clouds block the final swallowing of the sun, and it's time we turn our back on the water and return to civilisation. Pursued by the clouds and led by a stray dog, we reach the canopy of an empty restaurant just moments before the rain returns with an added ferocity to be expected at the edge of the world. ●

LAURISILVA
Home to trees that predate human activity on Madeira, the *laurvisilva* is a subtropical relic of a previously widespread laurel forest, which covered much of southern Europe 15-40 million years ago. Mainly composed of evergreen trees and bushes with flat, dark green leaves, the forests display a treasure of ecological niches and intricate food webs, and are home to many endemic species of flora and fauna. The *laurisilva* is found at altitudes between 300m and 1300m and thrives where the moisture brought by the trade winds condenses into dramatically beautiful V-shaped valleys. Preserved due the inaccessibility of the terrain and now under protection by UNESCO World Heritage Site status, the *laurisilva* still covers around a fifth of the island's surface and is the largest forest of its kind in the world.

PONTA DO PARGO
32°48'50"N, 17°15'45"W

in town for the lofotfiske

The lofotfiske | Escaping the elements at Anita's Sjømat | The surfers of Unstad

WORDS & PHOTOS:
HOLLIE HARMSWORTH & JON HAYWARD

Lofoten is a magnificent archipelago stretching like a wall into the Norwegian sea. The E10 road weaves through the islands via cantilever bridges and tunnels cutting through the highlands, joining up tiny islets and connecting the rural communities. The scenery is breathtaking and imposing: towering mountains jut straight out of the ocean, their craggy peaks looming like giants over colourful fishing villages that cling to the sides of deep fjords.

To the outsider, it would be easy to romanticise life on the islands being one of peace and tranquillity, hidden away from the rest of the world. But for over 1,000 years this land and its people have thrived off a world-famous fishing season, known as the *lofotfiske*. Perfectly positioned in the gulf stream, the sea comes alive in the winter with *skrei* (cod) migrating from the Barents Sea ready to spawn. Take a walk around one of the charming villages today and it is clear to see this old livelihood still plays a vital part in the lives of the islanders.

> "tourism is changing these islands but there is local determination to find a balance where both industries can prosper side by side"

Alongside the fishery, new industries are developing as a seasonal migration of another kind takes place each summer. Tourism is changing these islands but there is local determination to find a balance where both industries can prosper side by side.

cosy cafes and fishing villages

We know that by heading to Lofoten at the beginning of spring, we're taking a gamble with the weather. We pictured a continuous golden hour, candy pink skies and the northern lights dancing above the mountains in the night sky. However, things don't always play out like that – on a number of occasions we find ourselves in search of a shelter to hide from the elements. And when the rain comes in, there seems no better place to be than tucked up in a cosy café enjoying fresh coffee and waffles.

We experience a particularly icy downpour on the small island village of Sakrisøy. Among the fish racks and Rorbu cabins, we stumble upon Anita's Sjømat, a café, store, and processing facility – the very spirit of 'catch it, cook it, eat it'. The smell of smoked salmon greets us as we step inside and cast our eyes over chilled cabinets filled with halibut, shrimp and crab, presented with a

flair of artistry. Stockfish hangs from the wood-panelled walls next to dried seaweed and oilskin hats. The contemporary decor reveals a pride in the islands' centuries' old industry with black-and-white fishing photographs, antique tackle and two remarkable stockfish chandeliers.

SHELTER FROM THE STORM

We order two "world famous" fish burgers at the counter, hang up our wet gear and find a snug corner in which to see out the storm. Gazing out over the Reinefjorden, we watch small fishing boats heading in and out of the harbour, hungry gulls swooping down for a catch of their own.

Being able to stop and appreciate our surroundings gives us a chance to get a real sense of the place. As photographers, constantly chasing the light, how often have we raced through a village and missed out on moments like this?

▲ Above: A cosy respite.
▶ Right: Stockfish chandeliers at Anita's Sjømat.

ANITA'S SJØMAT
67°56'30"N, 13 6'41"E

HISTORY OF THE RORBU

Lofoten's famous Rorbu cabins – seasonal fishing cabins built on stilts along the coast, often painted red – date back to the 1100s when King Øystein commissioned them to be built for the *lofotfiske*. They were simple structures, built to provide shelter and storage for food and equipment, the poles allowing the fishermen easy access to their rowing boats on the sea. The cabins' red colour was not a design choice, rather the cheapest option as the paint was made by mixing ochre and cod liver oil. The name 'Rorbu' is believed to be a combination of the Norwegian words *ro*, which translates as 'to row', and *bu*, which means 'small house' or 'living place'. Today the Rorbu have become an iconic symbol of the Lofoten Islands and are more commonly used as authentic heritage accommodation for visitors.

lofotfiske

To witness *lofotfiske* (the fishing season) — the very foundations this island community was built on — is a treat on the senses. Travelling through each fishing village, we watch people building wooden drying racks called *hjell*, which are often masterfully assembled on the tops of sharp rocks. At the start of our trip many of the *hjell* are empty; but by the end of the week are full of *skrei*, — bundles of heads and fillets hung to dry in the arctic air, the perfect climate for producing stockfish.

Stockfish is an important part of Norway's cultural heritage and has been exported since the Viking era. It is still one of the world's most valuable sources, and the stockfish produced from Lofoten has Protected Geographical Indication (PGI) status. Over the years the process has hardly changed and for many islanders, it is still their main income. When the season starts, everyone gets involved, even the youngest have their role — cutting out the tongues of the *skrei*, which are highly desirable in the Norwegian food industry.

Although we had not intentionally planned our visit to coincide with the *lofotfiske*, we could not have timed it better. We can feel the buzz and energy, watching fishing boats heading out to sea and hauling in their catch, the sounds of timber being knocked together to make the drying racks, and the strong scent of drying *skrei*. To the locals, we are told, that is the sweet smell of money.

> "by the end of the week the hjell are full of skrei – bundles of heads and fillets"

powered by nature

Driving along the coast, it's hard not to stop every five minutes to take in the views. The beaches on Lofoten are some of the most spectacular we've ever seen. With long stretches of smooth, white sand and turquoise blue waters, set to a background of snow-capped mountains; even on a bitterly cold day it's an inviting landscape. It does seem odd to find such perfect beaches in the Arctic, but perhaps even more surprising is seeing the folks who pull on wetsuits and grab their boards to ride the icy waves.

We head up to Unstad beach, the surf centre of Lofoten, to see if we can spot some of these extreme surfers in action. The frozen sand crunches under our feet and the air bites at our exposed skin. No way will anyone be out in this, we say, before spotting four heads bobbing around in the waves. We linger for an hour or so, watching the surfers catch wave after wave. In the end, it is us that give in to the cold and we make our way back to the warmth of the car to thaw out our numb hands.

The power of nature is embraced wholeheartedly on Lofoten, connecting all who live and work here. But as more people are drawn to these islands – from fishermen and surfers to culinary connoisseurs – the impact on the environment and culture begins to show. Developing and prioritising sustainable tourism is now an ongoing mission of the Norwegian government, tourist board and the islanders themselves.

HIKING TO RYTEN

Ryten is a summit on the northwest of Moskenesøya and is one of Lofoten's classic mountain trails. The route takes in a magnificent view over Kvalvika beach and surrounding peaks, and is a real 'must-do' when visiting the islands. The hike begins near the village of Fredvang and takes you across a meadow before climbing up through the valley and into the mountains. Continuing the climb, you will pass some small lakes and navigate rocky terrain before the main ridge of the mountain comes into view. The final section is a steep climb up to the summit, but utterly worth it for the spectacular view across the fjords. You can do this hike throughout the year and it takes 3-6 hours, depending on the season and conditions. Consideration must be taken when attempting it in winter and spring as snow will cover the paths and navigation will be harder. For all hikes, dress appropriately and be prepared for quick changes in the weather.

postcard from the edge

Life on Britain's most remote island | All aboard
the *Good Shepherd* | The knitters of Fair Isle

WORDS: **OLIVER BERRY**
PHOTOS: **FINN BEALES**

It's dusk on the north coast of Fair Isle, and I'm besieged by puffins. They're everywhere: squabbling along the clifftops, gliding unsteadily in the stiff sea breeze, waddling boozily between their burrows among the bracken and gorse. I've never seen so many puffins in one place – nor experienced any that seem quite so utterly unfazed by my presence. They're happily standing within a few feet of me, ruffling their feathers as they jostle for position along the bluff. And I'm the only person here sharing the sunset with them.

Fair Isle has long been famous for its birdlife. This remote speck of rock, 3½ miles long and 1½ miles wide, marooned in the middle of the North Atlantic, harbours an astonishing variety of birds, some migratory, some resident: from European storm petrels, great skuas, fulmars and Arctic terns to puffins, cormorants and guillemots. More than 350 individual species have been recorded here, including 27 recorded nowhere else in the British Isles, and the island's bird wardens maintain one of the oldest ornithological records in Britain.

Fascinating though they are, it's not the birds that have drawn me to Fair Isle. It's the isolation. Twenty-four miles from the southernmost tip of Shetland, 27 from Orkney – Fair Isle is officially the remotest inhabited island in Britain, as far as you can get from anywhere else in the British Isles and still find someone to say hello to.

Like many people, the first time I heard of Fair Isle was thanks to its world-famous knitting pattern – a staple of so many socks, sweaters

> "as a student of faraway places, i've long wondered what life was like on this rocky atlantic outpost"

and Christmas scarves. But I also know its name from the Shipping Forecast – that peculiarly British radio broadcast that's part weather announcement, part soothsayer's riddle, part surrealist tone poem. As a student of faraway places, I've long wondered what life was like on this rocky Atlantic outpost: how its residents survive there, what drew them to such an isolated corner of Britain, and perhaps more importantly, what inspired them to stay.

There are two ways to get to Fair Isle. In good weather, it's a quick, 25-minute hop in a tiny eight-seater prop plane from Shetland. When the weather's bad, however – as it so frequently is in the North Atlantic – the only option is to hitch a ride aboard the *Good Shepherd IV*, a stout, steel-hulled vessel that doubles as

▶ *Good Shepherd IV*'s skipper Ian Best.
▼ Fair Isle has just one tarmac road that runs the length of the island.

the island's ferry and freight boat. Built for sturdiness rather than style, the boat runs three times a week from Lerwick on Shetland – it's usually a 2½-hour crossing, although it can take considerably longer when the weather takes a turn for the worse.

The man in charge of the *Good Shepherd IV* is Ian Best, a gruff, born-and-bred Fair Islander with a dry sense of humour. "Aye, the crossing can be a bit of an adventure," he says with characteristic understatement, sipping from a mug of tea as his crew unloads cargo on to the quayside at North Haven. "We sail in pretty much all weathers, so it can get a little hairy. But the boat's vital for the island; it's our link to the outside. We carry everything that can't come in by air: food, machinery, vehicles, building materials. Last week we brought over a BT engineer's van and the blades for the island's new wind turbines. A few times a year we ship flocks of sheep over to market on Shetland. That's a sight."

The current *Good Shepherd* has been in service since 1986, and is owned and operated by the Shetland Islands Council. The post of skipper is one of the most important on Fair Isle – it takes years to learn to navigate the island's rocky, reef-lined coastline, responsible for hundreds of shipwrecks. "It's a wild place, no doubt about that," Ian says, finishing his tea. "Unpredictable. You're never sure what the weather's going to do here, what surprises the island is going to throw at you. But that's what I love about it. Out here, we're living on the edge."

ENJOY THE SILENCE

Leaving Ian at the quayside, I set off across the island on foot. At 3½ miles long, it's possible to walk from one end of Fair Isle to the other in a couple of hours. Hiking along the island's sole tarmacked road, its stark, treeless landscape unfolds ahead – sloping fields, drystone walls, moors cloaked in purple heather, black cliffs tumbling into foaming surf. Flocks of sheep graze

on the uplands; great skuas (known on the island as bonxies) dive-bomb me as I walk past, protecting their nests in the undergrowth. I pass the island's tiny school (current pupil count: four) and its only shop, Stackhoull Stores. Occasionally, a white-walled croft house appears along the road, framed by fields, vegetable plots and patched-up polytunnels. Slowly, my ears tune in to the island soundtrack: surf-boom, gull-cackle, sheep-bleat, wind-whine. In between, the silence is overwhelming.

"The quiet takes getting used to, that's for sure," laughs Tommy Hyndman, an artist who occupies a white-walled house called Auld Haa, once the laird's residence, now Tommy's home and a B&B. Like many islanders, Tommy wasn't born on Fair Isle, he's originally from upstate New York, having moved here after hearing about a vacant croft on a news report on the radio. "For me, the wildness and isolation was the attraction. Back home, I felt my life was becoming too conventional. Moving here was an artistic statement as much

SHETLAND BIRDS

Tammie norie: *puffin*
Bonxie: *great skua*
Skooty alan: *Arctic skua*
Tirrick: *tern*
Maa: *herring gull*
Rippick maa: *kittiwake*
Swaabie: *great blackbacked gull*
Peerie swaabie: *lesser black-backed gull*
Peerie maa: *common gull*
Loom: *guillemot*
Sea craa, wilkie: *razorbill*
Whaap: *curlew*

"the shaw family maintains their croft while, like nearly all fair islanders, holding down a bewildering multitude of jobs"

as a life adventure." Tommy now lives alone at Auld Haa; his son Henry, who grew up on the island, returns as regularly as he can from university.

Further south along the island road, the Shaw family maintains their croft while, like nearly all Fair Islanders, holding down a bewildering multitude of jobs. Deryk Shaw works as a deckhand on the *Good Shepherd*, and is also a part-time fireman and occasional ground-crew at the airport. His wife Hollie runs her own clothing business, working with the island's community of knitters to produce the sweaters, scarves, gloves and hats for which the island is renowned. Their youngest children, Raven and Ythan, are completing their studies on the mainland – as there is no secondary school on Fair Isle – and come home every few weekends.

"It's an amazing place for kids to grow up," Hollie says, raising her voice over the whirr of her loom. "They have the place to themselves; this huge island playground. But there are hardships,

too: fewer friends, going away for school, the sense of isolation."

"And no cinema," adds her daughter Raven mischievously, as she heads out into the fields to round up the sheep, crook in hand, followed by her trusty sheepdog, Kes. In a matter of a few minutes, the sheep are penned, and she's headed home for supper. "Even though I get frustrated with it sometimes, I do love the island," she says, sitting on the croft's granite step.

Shades for Spindrift and Double Knitting

the knitters of fair isle

Kathy Coull

For hundreds of years, Fair Isle has been famous for its knitting. Composed of alternating coloured stripes and geometric shapes, the Fair Isle pattern shares similarities with traditional Scandinavian designs, a reminder of the maritime trade which once thrived across the North Atlantic.

Traditionally, all women on the island would have learned to knit by making clothes for their own families, with techniques and designs passed from mother to daughter. Knitting skills began to dwindle in the late 19th century with the introduction of mass-produced clothing, but has recently enjoyed a renaissance with several knitting collectives now spread out across the island.

"I can hardly keep up with the orders," laughs Kathy Coull, owner of the Fair Isle Textile Workshop. A passionate teacher and knitting historian, Kathy is one of the few knitters on Fair Isle that still produces her clothing entirely by hand (including spinning yarn from her own sheep). "It's so important to pass these skills on to the next generation. It's part of who we are as Fair Islanders."

The design might be ubiquitous, but there are a few rules that a true Fair Isle garment must follow. "Traditionally we would only use a few colours, and never

"it's so important to pass these skills on to the next generation. it's part of who we are"

more than two colours in a row," Kathy explains. "You can use the wool's natural pigments – brown, black, white and so on – or use dyes from plants such as madder, indigo, amphibious bistort and blocks (a Shetland term for the yellow iris). But these days knitters have access to many different of colours. The important thing to understand is that every garment has its own provenance: the Fair Isle design is very recognisable, but each knitter has their own interpretation of it. That's what makes each garment special."

"Growing up here, you don't really have friends; it's more like you're siblings. Realistically, I know I'll probably have to move away for a while, but I hope to come home and have my own family here one day. I want them to have the same experience I had."

I leave the Shaw's house and walk out along the west coast, tramping across green fields to the island's fissured edge. As I reach the cliffs, a line of crags stretches away into the distance, sheer and black, falling abruptly away into the Atlantic. Gulls and fulmars wheel in the spray, and a little way out to sea, a rock tower rises from the waves, its walls speckled white with the wings of thousands of seabirds. A seal pops its head out of the waves, then disappears with a flick of its fin. It feels like I'm standing on the edge of the known world, as it might have been marked on an old medieval map: the island feels raw, old, elemental – and suddenly very far away.

Fair Isle feels isolated enough now (the island only got 24-hour power

as recently at 2018 thanks to the installation of two new wind turbines), but it's almost impossible to imagine how remote it must have felt to its early settlers. Amazingly, people have lived here since Neolithic times – cairns and chambers tombs litter the island, along with many hill-forts, quarries and ancient kilns. Known as Fridarey to the Vikings – 'island of peace' – it's thought to have been inhabited for 5,000 years.

The island now has a population of just over 50 people, around a tenth of what it was in the early 19th century. Since 1955, the island has been owned and administered by the National Trust of Scotland (NTS), which acquired it from the Scottish stationer George Waterson – a passionate ornithologist and conservationist, who also built the first bird observatory on the island in 1948. Modern communications have made life here feel more connected, but it still feels remote in a way that very few corners of Britain now do.

Not that there's any shortage of people willing to live here, it seems

— the last time a croft on the island became vacant, the NTS received hundreds of applications. Would-be islanders are required to go through a rigorous selection process (priority is given to applicants with skills considered useful for the island, and to families with young children). Romantic as it may seem to escape to an isolated island, far from the stresses and strains of modern life, in reality, even the most enthusiastic arrivals often find life on the island challenging.

"Island life isn't for everyone," admits John Best, who served for many years as one of Fair Isle's ministers, and is now its oldest resident at the age of 84. "My wife took up a year's contract as the island's nurse in the 1970s, but somehow we never left. Other people only last a year or two here."

Now a widower and retired, John spends his time painting the island's coastline and working on community projects. "The most important thing here is to get involved. You simply can't survive on your own. You might not get on with everyone all the time, but when times are hard everyone pulls together," he explains, looking up from his canvas to watch the steady blink-blink of the island's South Lighthouse. "That's just what we do."

Never was this more apparent than during the devastating fire that consumed the island's bird observatory in 2019. On the night of the 10 March, the 'obs' – which doubled as the island's only hotel, restaurant, library and bar – went up in flames. Fair Isle's fire crew, all trained residents, turned out in the middle of the night to fight the blaze. "People help each other in times of need," John adds.

There are plans to rebuild the observatory as soon as 2022, but for now, he says, the islanders will do what they have always done: survive. "Living on an island forces you to live within your means," John explains. "That's what islanders here have always done. Life is stripped to its essentials: family, nature, friendships, community. If you ask me, that's what life is really all about." ●

plan your adventure

MADEIRA

GETTING THERE AND AROUND
Despite a seafaring history, reaching Madeira by boat is now the reserve of cruise liners and cargo ships. Fortunately, Madeira airport is served by over 15 airlines with direct flights from across Europe. Flights from Portugal take 2 hours, while flights from London are 4 hours. Hiring a car is the best option if you intend to explore beyond the tourist bus routes. However, driving on Madeira is not for the faint-hearted, especially when facing traffic on the mountain roads. Local buses are the cheapest option and reach most parts of the island.

STAY
A Casa Estrelícia-Dourada Garcês, São Vicente
Enjoy a taste of farm life, sampling homemade Madeira wine while taking in the mountain view from the pool.

EAT
Cantinho da Serra, Santana
Traditional Madeira seafood and hearty broth dishes. Perfect to warm yourself after a damp day on the forest trails.

EXPERIENCE
Seixal Natural Pools
Enjoy the warmth of the Atlantic waters in the lava pools at Seixal.

RESPONSIBLE TRAVEL TIP
Markets outside of Funchal offer an interesting sample of island life and a chance to support local producers.

LOFOTEN

GETTING THERE AND AROUND
Norwegian Airlines and Scandinavian Airlines run direct flights from Oslo to Harstad/Narvik airport, which is 4.5hrs drive from Reine. There are car rental companies at the airport. Or you can get a train from Oslo to Bodø and cross on the ferry to Moskenes. Most of the islands are connected by bridges /tunnels, making car or bike the best option for getting around.

STAY
Fishermen Cabins
These iconic cabins (Rorbu) are found throughout the islands, complete with kitchens to cook up that freshly caught fish. **classicnorway.no**

Camping
There are several sites with great facilities, and most don't require pre-booking. **lofotenbeachcamp.no**

EAT
Anita's Sjømat:
Serves the world-famous Fish burger and has its own store, perfect for picking up Stockfish treats. **sakrisoy.no/seafood**

EXPERIENCE
Surfing
Arctic Surf provides all levels of coaching, from beginner to advanced. It also has a hot tub! **unstadarcticsurf.com**

RESPONSIBLE TRAVEL TIP
Please don't trespass on private land – stick to trails and paths when hiking.

FAIR ISLE

GETTING THERE AND AROUND
Flights are operated as part of the Airtask Group Inter Islands Air Services (**airtask.com**). There is at least one flight a day in summer, weather permitting, leaving from Tingwall on Shetland. One flight each Saturday departs from Sumburgh. Bookings can be made by telephone (01595 840246) or email (lwk.ops@airtask.com). An alternative is to cross on the *Good Shepherd IV*, operated by Shetland Ferries (**shetland. gov.uk/ferries**). The boat usually sails three times a week from Shetland.

STAY
Since the fire at the Fair Isle Bird Observatory, the only option is B&B. Several islanders offer accommodation, including Kathy Coull at Upper Leogh (**kathycoull.com**) and Tommy Hyndman at Auld Haa (**fair-isle.blogspot.co.uk**). Find a full list at **fairislebirdobs.co.uk**.

EAT
There are no cafes or restaurants so you'll be buying supplies from Stackhoull Stores or eating with your accommodation host.

EXPERIENCE
Spot puffins
Head up to the cliffs of South Haven, a short walk uphill from the harbour.

RESPONSIBLE TRAVEL TIP
All rubbish has to be transported off Fair Isle, so minimise waste as much as possible. Bring your own water bottle.

back issues

Build up your collection by visiting our online store
ernestjournal.co.uk/store

ISSUE TWO
Britain's last oak tannery; surgeon John Hunter and the Irish giant; ghost villages; the murky origins of porter; the piano restorers; Canada's tiny homes.

ISSUE THREE
Wild man mythology; Victorian diableries; denim and the American frontier; slow adventures in Scilly; Brutalism; terrariums; Iceland's Huldufólk.

ISSUE FOUR
Ghost radio; adventures in Greenland; a darker side to tintype photography; the micro-nation of Sealand; the psychology of polar exploration.

ISSUE FIVE
The unruly world of made-up languages; experiments with time; cryonics; Vancouver Island's wild side; solargraphy; mountain bothies in Scotland.

ISSUE SIX
England's last Vikings; the Galápagos Islands; seafaring vernacular; hidden artists' studios; in the footsteps of George Mallory; aurora borealis in Snowdonia.

ISSUE SEVEN
Bread making in space; mapping Antarctic women; the immortal jellyfish; the absurd travels of the Kearton brothers; the evolution of sea charts.

ISSUE EIGHT
Rewilding in Romania; shanty boats; the peculiar world of bee etiquette; Snowdonia's mountain haunts; adrift in the Atlantic; otherworldly sand dunes.

ISSUE NINE
Life on the Blasket Isles; living art with David Nash; whistling languages of the world; a score designed to play for a thousand years; the bird men of Faroe.

a creative pause

During lockdown, photographer **Jim Marsden** trod the same path every day. The more he walked the path, the less aware he was of walking, and the more aware he was of thinking. The path became his place to pause, and his space to think.

WORDS & PHOTOS: **JIM MARSDEN**

Have you ever sat and watched Wallace and Gromit's *The Wrong Trousers*? Aside from a shady penguin named Feathers McGraw and some problematic techno-trousers, it contains the greatest chase sequence ever filmed. During the chase, the hero Gromit is in pursuit of Feathers while atop a speeding toy train. But he sees disaster in the distance; the track ends and Feathers is sure to escape. As he hurtles towards the end of the line, he spies a box labelled 'TRACK' up ahead. Scooping it up as he races past, Gromit hangs perilously over the front of the speeding train, laying new sections of track from the box in a blur, averting disaster to continue the chase.

I see my job and the work I do as that hastily laid track. On this track I keep my own train rolling forward that carries my family, the bulk of my relationships and my identity as a photographer. Each week I try to find enough track to fill the box. Enough track to lay down in front of my train and keep it rolling forward. But in the middle of March this year I ran out of track. I looked into the box. I tipped it upside down. I took it near the window so I could squint into the bottom of it, but the box was bare. I could see no more track.

I'd come to a hard-braking, squeaky-bum, full-stop. The track had run out because a new and awful virus was seeping dispassionately through society. I was told by the people who run our country to stay at home, and in doing so help stop the spread of it. Stop. Stay at home. Not in a holiday kind of way, the kind where you're just taking a rest but you'll be back in a week. It was the kind where I didn't know when I'd be going back. It might be two weeks, it might be two months. And late at night

when hope and positivity went to sleep and left me alone with fear and despondency, I realised it might even be never. A definite full-stop.

But stop is too final, too brick wall for me. My glass is always half-full and I believe in the blue sky behind the darkest of clouds. So rather than stop, I decided this was a pause. A pause is different. A pause is a pullover to the side of the road with your flask and sandwiches knowing you can rejoin the traffic. A pause is within a journey, a stop is the end. So if I could think of this as a pause, how could I use this time to pause well?

A CHANGE OF MINDSET

In November 2019 I met with the author Rob Poynton at his home in Madrid, not knowing then how relevant our meeting would be to this strange time. "A pause is a curious thing," he said. "It seems so simple and familiar; yet dwell on it for a moment or two and you start to realise that there's more to it than meets the eye."

Rob has thought a lot about the pause. In 2019 he published *Do Pause: You are not a To Do list* and filled its pages full of reflections on why we pause, pause as a tool and how we can pause well. He wrote about how our mindset wrongly puts the pause in opposition to doing, when it's really just as important, and about the challenge of finding time in our busy lives: "If making time to do things is difficult, making time to think is even harder. To think well involves more than intellect. We think with our hands and our hearts, we think by moving, we think by making. We each think in different ways and we think together in conversation. Our normal environment doesn't

"Our discomfort with any lack of doing may be the lack of pause 'heroes' in our western, industrialised culture"

support this quality of thinking and, as a result, most of the time we are just reacting. Creating 'time out to think' takes care and attention." Reflecting on this conversation, I realised the pause is time to think. A time to be embraced rather than endured. A gift.

Within the pause I couldn't work and, like many people, my work is part of my identity. I am Jim. I am photographer. It frames me so others can see the shape of who I am. But when the work vanished and I was told to stay at home, I didn't need the identity of photographer. Because at home I'm not a photographer. At home I am a husband to my wife, dad to my son and a dog called Ted. We form identities to serve roles, each arising due to circumstances and conditions. When we cling to identity we struggle. If I tried to be a photographer at home, it wouldn't work. My wife wants a husband and my son wants a dad – they don't want a photographer. We need to be able to enter roles fully when needed, but take them off when they're not. The identities we create are not who we really are.

BECOMING HUMAN BEINGS

During the pause I became more comfortable with days filled less with doing and more with just being. Being slow. Being together as a family. Being here without worrying I should be somewhere else. Our discomfort with any lack of doing may be down to the absence of pause 'heroes' in our western, industrialised culture. We revere industrialists and entrepreneurs who work tirelessly to create empires of productivity. Tales of adventurers fill our books and history lessons; people straining at the leash to be some place other than where they were, and usually needing extraordinary mental and physical effort to get there. History's heroes are beacons of exertion and doing. But where are our heroes of being? Our idle idols?

We ran out of track, and we paused. We figured out how to be, rather than do. We hung one identity on the back of the door, and wore another that fit the time better. And when things started to change and familiar rhythms returned, we got back to some doing but kept hold of the being; and instead of taking the train, for a while we decided to walk. ●

into the unfathomed

A singular figure who bridged the gap between science and literature, Rachel Carson recognised that "it is not half so important to know as to feel". Within a decade, she would catalyse the conservation movement, introduce the word 'ecology' into common parlance and awaken the modern environmental conscience with her epoch-making *Silent Spring*. In an edited extract from *Figuring* – a history of women who have changed our understanding of the universe – Maria Popova introduces us to Rachel Carson.

WORDS: **MARIA POPOVA**

"The more clearly we can focus our attention on the wonders and realities of the universe about us, the less taste we shall have for the destruction of our race," a slight woman with intent eyes the colour of Mediterranean seawater declares with unassuming aplomb from behind a lectern a size too large. "Wonder and humility are wholesome emotions, and they do not exist side by side with a lust for destruction."

This is not the wishful thinking of a naïve idealist or the shrill cry of an alarmist, but a clarion call by the nation's most respected science writer, who has taken the podium to deliver her acceptance speech for the John Burroughs Medal, and who would posthumously earn her country's highest civilian honour – the Presidential Medal of Freedom.

By the time Rachel Carson was awarded the prestigious medal for excellence in nature writing in the spring of 1952, the unknown marine biologist – who had spent years working for the United States government's Fish and Wildlife Service – had risen to worldwide celebrity with her trailblazing book *The Sea Around Us*, published several months earlier – a lyrical serenade to the unseen world beneath the surface of the ocean.

In addition to the John Burroughs Medal, *The Sea Around Us* earned Carson the National Book Award and established her as a singular bridge figure between serious science and serious literature, with Galileo's rigour and Thoreau's poetic gift.

Within a decade, Carson would catalyse the conservation movement, introduce the word 'ecology' into the lay lexicon, and awaken the modern environmental conscience with her epoch-making *Silent Spring* – one of those rare books, like Kepler's *Astronomia nova*, Margaret Fuller's *Woman in the Nineteenth Century*, and Darwin's *On the Origin of Species*, that change history by changing the human mind itself.

A YEARNING FOR THE OCEAN

Although Carson made her name by writing about the oceans – she had authored three books about the sea by the time she emerged on to land with *Silent Spring* – she had beheld the ocean only in her mind's eye for the first two decades of her life. A solitary landlocked child, she spent her days roaming the woods of western Pennsylvania to revel in the fellowship of birds, insects, and flowers, all the while dreaming of the sea. One day, roaming the cliffs behind her family's farm, Rachel found a fossilised fish skeleton that sparked an electric longing to know how that mysterious marine creature had ended up a terrestrial ghost, where the ocean it inhabited long ago had gone, and what such swathes of time meant beside the shallow tidal marker of a human life.

One rainy August day during her senior year of college, Rachel Carson laid her eyes on the sea for the first time. She was journeying to the Marine Biology Laboratory at Woods Hole on Cape Cod – one of the first scientific institutions to regularly invite female researchers and scholars. The ocean would remain Carson's lifelong love. Her encounter with the spruce-lined seashore through a curtain of fog at dawn, a pristine and primordial scene, gave her a sense of what the young Earth must have looked like:

"There was nothing, really, for human words to say in the presence of something so vast, mysterious, and immensely powerful. Perhaps only in music of deep inspiration and grandeur could the message of that morning be translated by the human spirit, as in the opening bars of Beethoven's Ninth Symphony – music that echoes across vast distances and down long corridors of time, bringing the sense of what was and of what is to come – music of swelling power that swirls and explodes even as the sea surged against the rocks below…"

Carson grew up in a family bereft of means, always knowing she wanted to be a writer. A voracious reader since early childhood, she was 11 when her story 'A Battle in the Clouds' – a wartime tale inspired by a letter from her brother Robert – was accepted for publication in the wildly popular *St. Nicholas Magazine*. The young people's magazine was a platform for the early writings of such literary titans as Edna St. Vincent Millay, F. Scott Fitzgerald, E. E. Cummings and William Faulkner. Rachel was paid $3.30 for her story – a penny a word. At 11, she was officially a professional writer.

She kept submitting stories to *St. Nicholas*, which published several more by the time she graduated from high school. Her senior thesis, titled 'Intellectual Dissipation', admonished against the squandering of our most precious human faculty – the "thinking, reasoning mind". At the heart of her thesis was a conviction that would govern the remainder of her days – a deep faith in the power of great books to transform and ennoble, casting real literature as "something that would raise you a little higher than you were yesterday, something that would make you willing and able for your part in the work of the world."

Decades later, Carson would mature into the recognition that "it is not half so important to know as to feel," for "if facts are the seeds that later produce knowledge and wisdom, then the emotions and the impressions of the senses are the fertile soil in which the seeds must grow."

A SYNERGY OF LITERATURE & SCIENCE

In the autumn of 1925, Carson enrolled in Pennsylvania College for Women in Pittsburgh with the intention of studying literature, aided by a $100 scholarship. But room and board cost another $575 – a Sisyphean financial push for the Carson family. Her mother made ends meet by giving piano lessons. Determined to give her daughter the education that would free Rachel from ever having to depend on a husband, Mrs Carson took on more students, then sold all her china. When one of Rachel's classmates came to dine with the family, she was taken aback by being served on the kind of plastic dishes given away as promotional gimmicks by cereal brands. Suspended by so tenuous a thread of opportunity, Rachel brought to scholarship an obsessive work ethic, aided by her mother, who came for regular visits and invested hours in typing up her daughter's papers. Introverted and besotted with books, Rachel spent her scant free time not socialising with her young peers, but in the company of guiding spirits long gone. She loved Milton and Shakespeare. She cherished Melville and especially admired Twain for his "hatred of hypocrisy." A colleague would later recall that "there was something about her of the 19th century." Throughout her life, Carson would keep by her bedside a copy of Thoreau's journals, which she would read as a "pleasant ritual" at night.

"it is impossible to understand man without understanding his environment"

As intentional as Carson was about the direction of her college education, the most significant event of her intellectual and emotional development arrived the way most transformative things enter our lives – through the back door of the mansion of our plans.

Consumed with the demands of her English major during her freshman year, Rachel had put off the curriculum's science requirement. At the start of her sophomore year, she enrolled in an introductory biology course taught by Professor Mary Scott Skinker. The tall, glamorous Professor Skinker was an uncompromising educator. Her students worshipped her – she seemed like an apparition from another era. On Saturdays, she came to dinner in elegant formal wear, with a flower pinned to her waist or her chest – a new species every week – which the girls assumed came from some mysterious suitor. On weekdays, she delivered enthralling lectures on natural history and evolution that awakened in her students an awareness of the glorious interleaving of all life and seeded a novel understanding of the continuity of existence – the present day was not a sealed jar adrift on the river of time, but a cabinet containing fossils of every single day that preceded it.

At 19, Rachel was as taken with this revelatory view of life as she was with the beguiling biologist. Under this dual bewitchment, Rachel changed her major from English to biology. As she continued writing for the university's student magazine, she began spending blissful hours dissecting specimens in the tiny laboratory atop the ivy-festooned three-story brick building that housed classrooms, dormitory rooms and the university's art studio.

At the intersection of science and literature, Carson found a focal point for the beam of her searching and sensitive intellect. "I have always wanted to write," Rachel told her lab partner late one night in her formaldehyde paradise. "Biology has given me something to write about."

This was the inception of Carson's lifelong conviction that literature and science live in vital symbiosis in illuminating the nature of reality, which she would articulate a quarter century later in her National Book Award acceptance speech:

"The materials of science are the materials of life itself. Science is part of the reality of living; it is the what, the how, and the why of everything in our experience. It is impossible to understand man without understanding his environment and the forces that have molded him physically and mentally. The aim of science is to discover and

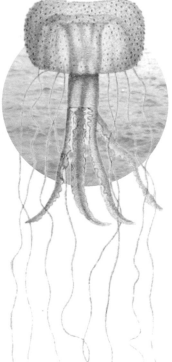

illuminate truth. And that, I take it, is the aim of literature, whether biography or history or fiction; it seems to me, then, that there can be no separate literature of science."

This may seem like an obvious truth today, but in 1926 it was a countercultural notion.

After Carson graduated, Skinker encouraged her to apply for a fellowship at Woods Hole. She fortified the encouragement with a formal recommendation that opened the gate to the prestigious Marine Biology Laboratory for her protégée, who was granted an eight-week fellowship. Freckles constellated Carson's skin as she spent hours under the August sun, bent over the tide pools swarming with astonishing life-forms – an experience that planted the seed that would blossom into *The Sea Around Us* more than two decades later.

ROMANCE UNDER THE WATERS

Over the next few years, Carson immersed herself in the science of the seas. To pay her way through the master's program, she took jobs as lab assistant and biology instructor – the only female one in the department – before graduating with a degree in zoology in 1932 and entering a PhD program at Johns Hopkins.

She applied for a low-level position at the United States Bureau of Fisheries and was hired as a field aide for $6.50 a day. When her supervisor noticed her literary gift, he tasked her with writing short scripts for the government agency's program *Romance Under the Waters* airing on CBS Radio. Meanwhile, she began submitting longer pieces about marine life to the *Baltimore Sun*, which, arrested by so uncommon a fusion of science and lyrical prose, made her a regular contributor to its *Sunday Magazine*.

Thanks to a series of civil service exams that Skinker had encouraged her to take, Carson qualified for a full-time position as a junior aquatic biologist. Impressed with her work on the radio scripts, Carson's boss tasked her with writing "something of a general sort about the sea" to introduce the bureau's work to the popular reader, expecting that she would summarise the agency's scientific research and annual reports. Instead, she transmuted the facts of science into something so lyrical that her chief told her – "with a twinkle in his eye," she would later recount – that it didn't work as a government report. But he encouraged her to submit it to *The Atlantic Monthly* as an essay.

Carson submitted her essay to the *Atlantic*, where it was published in the September 1937 issue as 'Undersea'. In this unprecedented masterpiece, she invited the reader to explore the most enigmatic recesses of Earth from the perspective of nonhuman creatures. To sense this world of waters, we must shed our human perceptions of length and breadth and time and place, and enter vicariously into a universe of all-pervading water.

"she transmuted the facts of science into a kind of poetry"

It was a revelation that science could be a literary subject, that it could speak – nay, sing – to the common reader with melodic might, so gracefully and graciously rejecting the false trade-off between the authority of science and the splendor of literary art.

WHERE SPLENDOUR DWELLS

Within a week, an envelope from the editor in chief of Simon and Schuster arrived at Carson's desk, inviting her to expand the essay into a book. *Under the Sea-Wind* was published four years later – a series of lyrical narratives about the life of the shore, the open sea, and the deep oceanic abyss. Determined to avoid the human bias of popular books about the ocean, which had always been written from the perspective of a human observer – a fisherman, a deep sea diver, a shore wanderer – Carson explored the three areas of marine life through the perspective of a particular, personified creature, christened by the scientific name of its genus.

Three decades before the primatologist Jane Goodall was ridiculed for giving chimps names during her pioneering studies of primates – work that later humbled our anthropoarrogance by revolutionising our understanding of nonhuman consciousness – Carson writes of Silverbar, the sanderling soaring in migration from the Arctic Circle to Patagonia; Scomber, the Atlantic mackerel journeying from New England to the Continental Shelf; and Anguilla, the eel on a voyage to spawn with millions of his kin in the abysses of the Sargasso Sea south of Bermuda. Out of this rich personified narrative emerges the book's central hero: the ocean itself.

In the spring of 1950, Carson arrived at the title for the book she had been incubating her entire life: *The Sea Around Us*. By the time she completed the book, Carson had scoured hundreds of technical papers, corresponded with scores of specialists, worked with dozens of librarians to find obscure documents and rare books on oceanography, and consulted more than a thousand different printed sources. All of this she distilled into what may best be described as a book-length prose poem about the science of the sea. On Monday 2 July, *The Sea Around Us* was published into a world already abuzz with excitement after its electric debut in *The New Yorker*.

Carson accomplished the improbable feat of enchanting lay readers and scientists alike. Twenty days after its publication, *The Sea Around Us* entered the *New York Times* best-seller list at number five, then steadily ascended to number one, where it was to remain for more weeks than any other non-fiction book ever had. *The Times* chose it as the outstanding book of the year. By the end of December, a quarter of a million copies had been sold. The publisher, who had failed to anticipate the book's success, struggled to keep up, going through six strained printings as book buyers complained about the shortage and readers added their names to months-long waitlists. With 15 years of magazine writing under her belt and a decade after the publication of her first book, Rachel Carson was declared an overnight success. ●

This is an edited extract from *Figuring* (Canongate, 2020), a history of women who have changed our understanding of the universe, by Maria Popova, the creator of Brain Pickings.

go there,
be there

There is an oft-used comic image of the family outdoors, portraying an
enthusiastic father leading a bedraggled and weary family on a country walk.
The father marches on, full of vim and vigour with only the destination in
mind, while his family trail despairingly behind. We laugh at the image, but for
some it contains grains of truth. Somehow our work ethic followed us from
the office – 'achievement' wormed its way into our time spent outdoors.

At Moorswood we think time spent outdoors should be different.
Our working lives can be so full of doing and busy-ness, that we need a little
time full of pause and quiet, to breathe and appreciate where we are.

So we made the Ramblers Roll, to help you pause. A portable square of
warm and dry ground for one, which neatly rolls up and fits in your bag
or pocket. For camping with friends, a quiet lunch in the field, a spot by
the river or even just a coffee break on a damp park bench. On your own
or with others, the Ramblers Roll helps you spend longer outside.

Our Ramblers Rolls are made with 100% natural fibres, from our own British shores.
A water resistant wax cotton base, lined with an organic wool felt for
warmth and comfort, topped with a hardy wool tweed or limited edition
artist print. Bound by stunning oak bark tanned leather or hemp straps.
They are all handmade in Devon with love and attention to detail.
A carefully considered design, with craftsmanship and longevity at its heart.

It's not always about where you're going, it's about where you are. So go
outside, leave work behind. And remember to sit and pause for a while.

moorswood.com

MW | MOORSWOOD

chasing aurora

From crossing lava fields in Iceland to enduring
subzero temperatures in Canada's bear country,
photographer **Rebecca Douglas** reflects on her
lifelong obsession with chasing the Northern Lights

WORDS & PHOTOS: **REBECCA DOUGLAS**

m y fascination with the night sky started on balmy summer evenings in my childhood. The Perseids meteor shower falls during the school holidays, and Dad used to set up sun loungers and duvets and we'd lie there for hours staring at the sky, gleefully pointing out the flashes of light.

This fascination continued into adulthood, but took a different turn from meteor showers. I am now obsessed with chasing aurora borealis, also known as the Northern Lights. Every chase is so exhilarating, and I never know what the night will hold. It's not without its challenges, particularly in subzero temperatures in the Arctic wilderness (down to -22C so far), when you're reminded of the fragility of the human body, and have to read signs in nature and know when to adapt your plans. But in the face of adversity you learn a lot about your own resilience.

Ultimately I think that dramatic build-up is what draws me into the awe and intensity of witnessing such an incredible celestial event. It is a total sensory experience – something that moves me to tears.

To find the truly dark spots, I'm often out in the far northern remotest corners of the globe, in the wee hours of the night. Undulating lava fields in Iceland, or ominous moonlit human-shaped silhouettes in the distance – it's easy to see how so many folk tales were born in these rugged landscapes that flirt with your imagination.

The enormity of the star-laden sky weighs down on me, putting an end to my internal chatter. It's often a

LOCATION IS EVERYTHING

There are a few key things you need to line up for optimum aurora chasing conditions. Firstly, you'll need clear skies – apps like windy.com are good at mapping cloud cover so you can plan your chase. You'll also need to be away from light pollution, and try to book your trip when there is a new moon, as weaker aurora can be overpowered by light from a full moon. When I'm chasing, I usually book accommodation on a day-by day-basis so I can move as and when to where the clear skies are. I love booking cabins in remote countryside, away from light pollution and urban areas. Hopefully you'll be blessed with all the right conditions – just wrap up warm, step outside and enjoy the display.

"the awe and intensity of witnessing such an incredible celestial event is something that moves me to tears"

▼ New Year's Eve 2016 in
Thingvellir National Park, Iceland

strange connection between letting go of fear of the unknown and being totally absorbed in the moment. But oh, how those moments can be abruptly interrupted by the unexpected, from fending off two lone farm dogs on a Faroese Island, one attached to each arm, to trying to collapse your tripod faster than the speed of light as you hear a guttural growl from the bushes in bear country. Nature reminds you of the fragility and beauty of life all at the same time.

The photos I take are a bonus that jog my memory of the story of the chase, who I shared it with and how I sometimes had to dig deep and push against challenging conditions to witness the aurora.

I will never forget the first time I saw the lights after waiting on the shores of the achingly beautiful Jökulsárlón in 2014. We waited for darkness for two hours in the car; the moon was full and framed with

a 22 degree halo. It was so bright it felt like daytime. After an hour of clear skies we watched clouds rapidly forming above the glacier. And then, what was this? My camera picked up a green arc in the gaps of the clouds but the moon was so bright it overpowered it. For a moment in clearer sky to the east, the arc of aurora pulsed for a few seconds – we all saw it, then it was gone. The sweet adrenaline rush of euphoria got us through the six-hour drive back to our cabin, but I knew I wanted to see it more for longer, to be with it.

I didn't know it at the time, but this first glimmer above the lagoon were the opening scenes of my adventures with the aurora. I now sit on the other side of eight frustrated attempts over six years, returning to the same spot to get conditions to align to finally see the aurora vividly above the icebergs. And with nearly 30 trips chasing across six countries and two continents, always learning and making

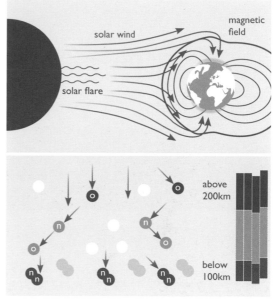

◀ After eight attempts, Rebecca finally managed to capture the spectacle above Jökulsárlón.

so many friends and memories along the way, it's my absolute joy to share a little more about the science and how to bring together a successful chase.

Sat in a bar in the middle of nowhere in Iceland, you can easily spot an aurora chaser a mile off – chain drinking coffee; scrolling space weather apps; camera batteries charging. I got chatting to Sigríður, a local guide who was staying up to keep an eye on the sky and wake her travellers if anything was happening. There's something so calming and captivating about stories told by Icelanders, particularly when they're telling you about the Northern Lights. "I always think – we're seeing aurora because the sun sent us some energy to excite our gas particles, and all the photons dance together. It's very special," she said. I took another sip of Boli (a great local beer) and let her gently delivered words soak in.

WHAT CAUSES THE AURORA?

As Sigríður said with such profound simplicity, the sun is a bubbling ball of plasma, and when solar wind and flares leave its surface they spread across space. It gets interesting when they're Earth-bound and hit our atmosphere and geomagnetic field, which protects us from this space weather. When charged particles from the sun strike atoms in Earth's atmosphere, they cause electrons in the atoms to move to a higher-energy state. When the electrons drop back to a lower energy state, they release a photon: light. And it is these transfers of energy in our atmospheric gases that give us the aurora. And as well as the northern lights, aurora borealis, there are also southern lights, aurora australis. The latter are seen much less frequently as land is sparse in the areas they're active.

The different colours depend on which gas particles have becomes charged in the atmosphere. The most common colour is a yellow-green, produced by oxygen molecules about 60 miles above the earth's surface. Much more rarely observed are the all-red auroras, which are produced by high-altitude oxygen, at heights of up to 200 miles above the Earth's surface. Nitrogen produces blue or purplish-red aurora.

The aurora I witnessed on Sunday 6 March 2016 (Mothering Sunday) was an incredible display, as the

"it was a milestone on a journey of grief and ever since, i've found it a very spiritual experience"

Earth's atmosphere took a direct hit from a significant solar flare and over the evening it gleamed in all the aurora colours. It was one of the few times I've seen reds and purples – it needs to be a particularly active aurora for that to happen. This was the night that got me hooked on aurora chasing. It was very poignant, too, as I'd recently lost both my gran and aunt (her daughter) three weeks apart, and this was my first Mother's Day without them. Their favourite colours were red and hot pink, and, as if in honour of them, those colours shone bright that night. On a day that we were celebrating our mothers, I felt as though they were all up there dancing with Mother Nature. It was one of those milestones on a journey of grief, and ever since, I have always found watching aurora a very spiritual experience. ●

PREDICTING THE AURORA

A lot of aurora apps mention a KP index with a range of 1-9. This is loosely helpful to forecast aurora, indicating there could be activity within a three-hour period. But a lot can happen in three hours so I use a combination of space weather and two apps to get more accurate real time information. I read space weather data from deep-space satellite DSCOVR – we know the sun's energy passing this takes around 15-60 minutes to arrive. This tells me the speed of the solar wind (km/s) – faster is better. I also check the plasma density p/cm3 – the denser the better. The Interplanetary Magnetic Field (IMF) has two measures, one is the overall strength nT (bigger is better) and the other is Bz, indicating the direction of the IMF and a negative -nT is better. The Glendale App (aurora-alerts.uk) is the most accurate app I've ever used. It gives real-time data with the substorm tracker, using magnetometers across the aurora zone, which measure how active the aurora is. By combining space weather data and using the Glendale App, I can time my chases down to the last sips of a flask of tea, it is that reliable! The second app I use is Live Aurora Network, which has a series of cameras in the aurora zone and is free to use. I can hop on and see what sky conditions are like if satellite maps for cloud cover are changeable, and this helps to make a decision on where to chase. Armed with this information, it's time to head out and see what the night will hold.

A Mother's Day heart from Mother Nature herself.

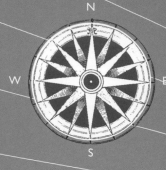

an ocean odyssey

Inspired by a trip to South Georgia, an inhospitable
island abundant in wildlife but with no permanent
human inhabitants, **Russell Arnott** explores
deserted whaling stations and delves deep into
ocean migrations both great and (very) small

WANDERING WHALES

"Reward paid for return to Discovery Committee Colonial Office London." I read the engraving on what appears to be an oversized brass drawing pin, mounted on the wall above my head. Almost 8,000 miles from the UK capital, I find myself pondering this artefact in the South Georgia Heritage Museum, nestled among the abandoned whaling station of Grytviken.

This pin is known as a whalemark; fired into the thick blubber of a whale and later recovered when whalers harpooned the poor creature. Whalemarks were an early attempt to track whale migrations. The intensity of whaling 100 years ago meant that most whalemarks were recovered within days of tagging, but the few whalemarks that were returned hinted that whales were able to cover vast distances across our ocean.

Seeking to better understand the geographic extent of whales, aquarist Charles Townsend took to the archived logbooks of whaling vessels, found in libraries and personal collections across New England, USA. Amassing the locations of over 50,000 whale kills, each was painstakingly charted on a world map as part a 1935 report entitled *Distribution of the Sperm Whale*, providing the first picture of just how widespread these animals were.

Thankfully, we no longer have to use whaling to understand whales. Fast forward to the modern day and scientists now find themselves with an array of technology at their disposal. From drones and hydrophones to digital tagging, scientists are slowly building up a picture of the movement of entire whale populations. In South Georgia, I get a chance to chat to whale biologist Dr Jen Jackson. "South Georgia was once the epicentre of modern whaling," she informs me. When Norwegian whaler, Carl Larsen (of Larsen Ice Shelf fame) landed in 1903, he proclaimed, "I see them in hundreds and thousands."

Throughout the early 20th century, the whaling stations of South Georgia slaughtered more than 175,000 whales. But why were there so many whales there to begin with? Jen theorises that South Georgia might act as a "motorway service station", where different whale populations stop off to feed before continuing to breeding, calving, and feeding grounds around the world. The story has been complicated by 19th-century sealers, who decimated the island's fur seal population prior to the arrival of the whalers. "As fur seals compete with whales for krill, it is possible that this lack of seals caused a shift in the ecosystem, causing whales to feed closer to the shore," suggests Jen.

In 2012, South Georgia was designated a marine protected area. Covering more than one million square kilometres, it is the fifth largest on Earth. As more ocean is granted this protection, many of these whale populations are slowly recovering; southern hemisphere humpbacks have seen a 70 per cent recovery – proof that sustained conservation efforts supported by science is having an effect.

South Georgia

North Carolina

TRAVERSING TURTLES

Whales are not the only marine creatures capable of covering vast distances. Having been on Earth since the time of the dinosaurs, the seven extant species of turtle are true living fossils. Coming ashore to nest, subsequent generations return to the same beach they were born on to also lay their eggs. How a sea turtle was able to locate its exact 'birth beach' remained a mystery. Turtle skulls have been found to contain high concentrations of magnetite crystals (an adaptation they share with many animals, including humans). As the turtle embryo grows, the magnetic field of the beach is imprinted on to the crystals, providing a permanent wayfinder, allowing the turtles to return to their point of origin. These same crystals also allow turtles to navigate across entire oceans.

One such story involves a malnourished loggerhead turtle that washed ashore in North Carolina, USA. Named Fisher by the local aquarium, the loggerhead was slowly rehabilitated until being released ten years later. The GPS tag placed on Fisher allowed researchers to monitor his progress. Instead of hitching a ride with the Gulf Stream, Fisher made a beeline (a turtle line?) for his birth beach on the Cape Verde islands; a year-long swim of over 11,000km, against the current. Turtle studies across the globe have reported similar feats of endurance as they span entire oceans foraging for food.

Recent research into how animals use magnetic fields has discovered specific groups of chemicals in turtle eyes. Now known as cryptochromes, these proteins have been seen to transfer electrons, producing a signal when in the presence of magnets. Could it be that turtles can actually see Earth's magnetic field?

"could it be that turtles can actually see earth's magnetic field?"

Cape
Verde

PADDLING PLANKTON

The Second World War saw the advent of
many technologies as each side tried to gain
an upper hand. As Hitler's U-boat submarines
continued to wreak havoc across the Atlantic,
Allied oceanographers scrabbled to invent
a method of detecting their underwater
adversaries. They eventually arrived at sonar,
a new technology that involved timing how
long a sound took to reflect off a submerged
object; as the operator knew how fast the
sound was travelling, it was possible to
calculate the distance to this object.

As the technology was rolled out across
the Allied navies, reports started to come
back that the sonar was registering the
seabed at a depth of 300 to 500m where
the charts expected depths of 2000, 3000,
4000m. Even weirder was the fact that this
false ocean bed was seen to be shallower at
night and deeper at daytime.

Sampling of this layer eventually
determined this "false bottom" was initiated
by some of the smallest animals in the sea;
a group of microscopic zooplankton called
copepods. A key component in the marine
foodweb, it was discovered that copepods

swim up to surface waters at night to feed
on phytoplankton (single-celled plants) while
avoiding detection from predators.

As the zooplankton began their nightly
migration, certain predators had discovered
their feeding strategy and duly chased the
mass of copepods upwards. The predators,
mainly lanternfish, were found to reflect
the sonar off their swimbladders; a gas-filled
organ that maintains buoyancy at depth.
Following the fish were audiences of deep-
sea squid (yes, that is the collective noun for
squid), also adding to the strength of false
bottom signal.

Subsequently termed the deep-scattering
layer by marine biologists, further research
showed just how sensitive to light the deep-
ocean is. The layer was seen to be deeper
under a full moon, quickly becoming
shallower when clouds obscured
the moonlight. And what is now
recognised as largest migration on
Earth, the copepods swim almost
2000m in a 24-hour period; the
human equivalent of a daily swim
from London to Lisbon.

fforest

We've been making some quiet changes here at fforest — changes that will pleasantly surprise our regular guests, and offer a world of wildness, yet comfort, to those who've never graced our farm, coast and town dwellings before.

DOWN ON THE FARM

On our farm we've created new Japanese-style bathhouses for our Onsen Domes, each of which sleeps up to four guests and comes complete with an outdoor kitchen, king-size bed and log-burning stove. Larger groups or families will be in the lap of luxury in our Garden Shacs, highly insulated to ensure a cosy autumn stay. And then of course, there's our Georgian farmhouse, stout as a cottage loaf but with all the swish of a ski lodge — the ideal place for gatherings all year round.

TO THE SEA

Just a short walk from Wales Coast Path and the National Trust-owned Penbryn beach are our Coast Cabins, many with sea views and cosily kitted with Welsh wool blankets and cushions. We also have our Coast Dome — a romantic getaway with a log-burner and rural views from the giant bay window.

INTO TOWN

In an old granary warehouse, just a stone's throw from Cardigan's vibrant High Street, are our converted lofts, all with a river view so you can spot wild geese, kingfishers and otters playing in the Teifi. The lofts are also close to our Pizzatipi, where you can enjoy stone-baked pizzas, great coffee and Welsh craft beers in the riverside courtyard.

We truly believe that Autumn is the best time for visiting this wild slice of Welsh coast — the beaches are quieter; the woodland walks are at their most beautiful; and there's an abundance of local produce for some delicious outdoor cooking. Here at fforest farm, coast and town, we provide you with a place to stay, play and dream in nature.

coldatnight.co.uk

What would Gwen do?

                    that blank hour

            scrambled

upwards to the skyline.

       grey fogs

Whenever photographer **Hazel Simcox** heads out to the mountains of North Wales, she often takes a particular book with her, not a guidebook, but a memoir. **Fern Scott** speaks to Hazel about the words of mountaineer Gwen Moffatt, and how they influence her experience, and images, of landscape

WORDS: **FERN SCOTT** | ARTWORK: **HAZEL SIMCOX**

the cliffs
strenuous,

unaware

primarily physical

In 1946, 21-year-old Gwen Moffat visited North Wales for a walking holiday. It was her first trip of this kind and it changed the course of her life. She fell in love with the mountains, and on her return, she was consumed with dreams of climbing the rock face again. A few months later, without any practical thoughts for the future, Gwen left her post as an army driver and headed back to North Wales with ambitions only to climb. She sustained herself with occasional odd jobs, and sometimes went for days without food, sleeping in the open air – all so that she could dedicate herself entirely to the mountains.

When Gwen began mountaineering, she was an outsider, knowing no one in the community and being one of very few female climbers, often garnering attention for her habit of climbing barefoot. She ultimately became Britain's first female mountain guide and in 1961 published a memoir of her experiences, *Space Below My Feet*, which made her an inspiration for generations.

More than 50 years later, photographer Hazel Simcox came across Gwen's memoir while avoiding the rain in a secondhand bookshop. Gwen's straightforward writing style and enthusiastic descriptions of her experiences and the landscapes instantly appealed to Hazel, and became not only the inspiration for but an integral part of her photography project 'Space ----- My ----'.

For her project, Hazel follows in Gwen's footsteps, exploring many of the places she visited, and combining beautifully balanced landscape photography from her own journeys with redacted selections of text from Gwen's memoir. Together the image and text create a reflection on Hazel's own experience.

I spoke with Hazel to share her insights into her creative process, her relationship with nature and all the ways Gwen's words feed into her life.

Has there always been a connection between being in nature and photography for you?
I felt that connection when I first got into photography as a teenager, but when I did my degree, landscape photography was considered a bit unusual – not quite what they expect you to do. Also, as a teenager, country walking wasn't really on my radar.

It wasn't until I was older that my interest in photography and nature aligned again. I felt I didn't know the British landscapes as well as I should, so started exploring the land around me. I quickly learned that to do this fully I would need to push myself physically. It took time for me to develop the knowledge and physical strength to explore the landscapes I wanted to. I soon developed an interest in climbing. All of this time outdoors intertwined with a new confidence in myself and my work, where I knew I just wanted to photograph the landscape and not care about what other people thought.

How did you begin to use literature as your guide to the mountains, and how did that evolve into the 'Space ----- My ----' project?
I was reading lots of different walking literature, such as Nan Shepard's *Living Mountain* and Rebecca Solnit's *Wanderlust*, which introduced me to new landscapes. I then began attending a workshop for emerging artists at an organisation called Grain, based in the Midlands.

During conversations at these workshops, people asked me why I was photographing the landscape, why I was going out walking and why I was bringing a book (*Space Below My Feet*, by Gwen Moffat) to the workshops. At the time, bringing the book felt like bringing a mate with me to keep me company. And then I realised that the book was the inspiration I needed and I couldn't ignore it. It all fell into place and made perfect sense.

"She was one of very few female climbers, often garnering attention for her habit of climbing barefoot"

bewildered

I don't remember making the decision to go

less tolerant

thinking calmed me down.

I teach photography and one of my students presented her findings on Dadaism to me. She told me that to make a Dada poem you take a page, cut out the words, shake them up in a hat, then pick them out one by one. As she spoke, I saw the books I'd been reading as individual words, rather than prose. This inspired me to revisit Gwen's text, play some games with it, and as such take ownership.

How do you use the inspiration from Gwen's literature to create your own experiences?
As much as the locations I'm photographing have some relation to where Gwen might have been, in no way am I trying to take on her exact pathway. The places I visit and the words I leave behind in my redactions are my honest reactions to the experience I had in the place that was linked to Gwen's journey.

Do you plan routes with photography in mind or does it happen naturally?
I don't always take my camera; I go on a lot of walks without it. I tend to take photos when I feel safest, even though some of the experiences I share in the text might not be about the safe moments. If I already know the route, I'm more likely to take the camera.

I have a love-hate relationship with my camera — I want to make the images, but it can be restricting at times. When I leave it behind I often regret it, but I think you have to do it to feel an element of freedom.

When you're taking a photograph, what is it you're trying to capture?
I guess I'm trying to capture the little moments that intrigue me. I'm always looking for isolated balances of tones and colour, a pattern of shade – light-based intrigue.

For me, walking frees my mind from all connections with society and culture, and that helps me be completely in the moment and see the basics of shapes, colours, patterns and textures. That's what I'm trying to photograph. I'm also just enjoying the view – they're not heavily deep in any concept!

How do you make your final selection of photos?
I go for the prettiest! Beautiful little moments where the light and environment balance to create an emotive image.

So there's no part where you're trying to choose something that captures a feeling you might have had?
Maybe there's some connection in my choice. I usually end up with about six potential images, and when I pair them with text I make a curatorial decision on which image relates best to the words. If the text mentions confusion I'll want the image to feel quite unclear, or if the text is about fear I want it to be slightly darker.

Tell us about your process of pairing the images with Gwen's words.
When redacting the text, I look at the words without actually reading the text. I highlight words that relate to my own experience and, as I'm highlighting them, it reminds me of the experience and sometimes things come through that I didn't expect. On a recent climb, my partner and I walked through a valley and for a while I couldn't hear him. In the text, Gwen also mentions that she couldn't hear her climbing partner in that same valley. I liked that we'd both experienced that same little moment.

I really enjoy the process of revisiting and redacting the text. It's like writing something new, but the words I work with are already fixed in the order they appear on the page. I can't add anything to it, and I can't change where they are going to be on the page.

"I have a love-hate relationship with my camera — I want to make the images, but it can be restricting at times"

beautiful and sophisticated.

A light   soft yellow

                                                    deep enough

        beam silently

long walks
caught in mist
ponderous

rushed
nothing outside.
grumbling

One of the nice things about using Gwen's words is that I'm limited in the narrative that I can tell. I don't have the chance to change the experience, but I get to relive it in a way that I don't plan. I'm reliving fragmented moments, and reflection makes you think about experiences differently.

Why does Gwen appeal to you?
It's very much her attitude and mindset that inspire me. I don't think modern readers are used to her style of writing – it's quite naive in some ways. I also like that in contrast to other adventurers, who seem quite serious, she was also interested in the social side of things – sleeping on the floor of shacks and drinking wine.

I love that she went headstrong into a new way of life – a very masculine way of life. She was the only female in a very male dominated environment. I admire that braveness in her. She also put familiar places in the adventure category for me. Her writing opened up North Wales into a new playground – it became more than just the familiar paths I already knew.

Are there any parts of her personality you try to emulate while you're out in the mountains?
I'm inspired by her ability to focus and deal with the task at hand, and the way she finds an element of enjoyment within that, whether it's before or after a big moment. Also, the way she sets her mind to something. She decides she is going to climb a route, and I can't imagine her stopping halfway up and whimpering because it's too frightening, which is what I do!

"I love that Gwen went headstrong into a new way of life – a very masculine way of life. I admire that braveness in her"

When I'm in those moments, I say to myself, "I really don't think Gwen would do that. What would Gwen do?"

'What would Gwen do?' seems like a common theme among her fans. Why do you think this is?
The phrase 'What would Gwen do?' was popularised by Alex Messenger of the British Mountaineering Club, who founded the Operation Moffat project. He used the phrase in a social media campaign about women's empowerment. That's how I use it in many ways.

There are not that many recognised female mountaineers. The famous ones tend to be extreme climbers. What I like about Gwen is that she is relatable and accessible. I think, as she was climbing 50 years ago, amateur climbers can par themselves with her then, but you can't really par yourself with the epic women climbers of today. The ability required for what she did isn't that far-fetched. You can go out and do all the climbs she did without being an extreme climber, but she was really progressive for her time. And she opened up the mountains to women.

She once commented, "I didn't climb hard, but I did climb well." And that's nice. I don't plan to climb hard. I just want to enjoy it.

How do you feel when you follow in Gwen's footsteps? Do you get a thrill knowing she has seen the same views you're looking at now?
I do. It's a shared experience. I'm not the kind of person who wants to find new routes or find trails that have not been trodden. I like to follow people's paths. I like to know what I've done has been done by others. There is often a lovely moment when I stop and see a view or look at a rock face, and think 'Gwen was here, she did this', and I find that reassuring. ●

You can see more of Hazel's 'Space ---- My ----' project at **hazelsimcox.co.uk.** *Space Below My Feet* by Gwen Moffat was originally published in 1961, and a new edition was released by W&N in 2013.

Buy Less. Buy Better.

The Roam Backpack. Crafted in Wales exclusively for
The Future Kept by Rural Kind. We donate 2% of all our sales to grass
roots organisations fighting for environmental and social justice.

thefuturekept.com

inventory II

WORKMANSHIP
POCKET SEASCAPES

When David Cass browses a flea market, he doesn't see piles of faded antiques – he sees canvasses. Rusting signs, old crates, drawers, even a copper bed-warming pan – these have all been surfaces for his seascapes, each lending a unique yet subtle texture and framing to the artwork. Each of his pieces carries an environmental message – he recently painted on reformed plastic from 1,500 used yogurt pots: "Our oceans need us more than ever," David says. "While the Earth has had some breathing space during lockdown, this had little impact on sea rise. One reason our world is warming – and ergo, our seas rising – is down to the production of petroleum products, such as plastics. Plastics that then go on to pollute oceans."

Just as an aside, we urge you to head over to David's website or Instagram feed to watch a short film of him painting a seascape on a matchbox. It's hypnotically satisfying. Visit **davidcass.art** and **@davidcass.art** on Instagram

WILD FOOD
NATURAL FUEL

A tricky business, snacking in the outdoors. We potter up the fells in search of unspoiled nature, but half the food in our lunch packs is stacked with sugar and palm oil, and encased in shiny plastic wrappers destined to be picked over by seagulls at a landfill site.

Outdoor Provisions makes a different kind of energy bar, aiming for a lower impact on the environment. The packaging is compostable, and the bars are natural and vegan, with no refined sugar. The flavours are inspired by our national parks – so think Cherry Bakewell for the Peak District, Bara Brith for Snowdonia, Kendal Mint Cake for the Lake District and Parkin for the Yorkshire Dales. A bit like stopping by the local bakery before you set out, except that by lunchtime the bars are still intact, rather than a mashed up wad at the bottom of your pack. outdoorprovisions. co.uk. Words: **Joly Braime**

WORKMANSHIP
MADE TO LAST

Good coats never die. The old ones live at the end of the coat rack nearest the door, unapologetically tatty and bedraggled. Even when beset by pressures from family to be rid of it, you can't bear to do it.

The lucky ones spend retirement in the garden with their pockets full of tissues and wrappers, worn in all the elements, hunched over honeysuckle and hydrangeas.

Since 2015 Wood & Meadow has been peddling all things beautiful from quality brands such as Pendleton, Sandqvist and Haeckels. While thoughts of making something under its own name wafted around, nothing seemed just the right thing. Until one sunny afternoon while idly daydreaming in their Lancashire garden, those hazy thoughts wafted towards crafting a coat. A coat you'd never want to get rid of, a coat that would get better with age, something beautiful. And could it actually be made here in Lancashire?

From this hazy musing followed a serendipitous journey through the county's making heritage to modern day makers. The remains of Lancashire's immense industrial past are still plain to see in the mills and factories that now lie quiet, but the skills and craft never left. Six months later and the first Wood & Meadow Work Jacket was born. A jacket of the worker and stroller and gardener alike, with a minimal, symmetrical silhouette, every bit of it designed and made in Lancashire.

Good coats never die. Good coats are still made in Lancashire. Who'd have thought? Sometimes you have to stand back to see the wood (and meadow) for the trees. Words: **Jim Marsden**

Wood & Meadow Work Jacket, check website for colours and price, **woodandmeadow.com**

In addition to her repertoire of carved spoons and Gumati brushes, Sophie Sellu of Grain & Knot has introduced a unique collection of vases, hand-hewn into an array of fondle-some shapes. We particularly like the ones with Polo mint-style holes through them.

Sophie, your pieces usually have a utilitarian or culinary element to them – what inspired you to make vases?
I have so many off-cuts from other work in my shed. They're often tiny and seemingly useless. I wanted to show the full potential of the pieces, while making something useful at the same time.

What inspires the unusual shapes? Do you usually have a shape in mind before you start?
I have a few shapes in mind beforehand - I usually start by drawing shapes on paper, then adapt them to the off-cuts, guided by the grain of the timber. I like to pair vases together, so it's fun working out which shapes sit well with others.

Your work has a very human element to it – you can see each piece has been hand-hewn. Is this a conscious decision in your work?
Yes, I think it's important to see the marks of production. It gives each piece a faceted surface and a very tactile feel.

What would you put in these vases?
The vases are only suitable for dried blooms, as they cannot hold water. I often put in things found on my walks. I always look forward to autumn as the changing colour of the leaves gives a wider variety of items to collect. It's quite a mindful process to slow down and notice the beauty in nature.
See more of Sophie's work at grainandknot.com

GEAR
CROSS-COUNTRY SWIMMING

Last time *Ernest* tried to assemble a raft for a wild swimming expedition, he'd forgotten his twine and had to make do with thin strips of venison jerky. The thing disintegrated as soon as it hit the water, but the jerky made a moist and consolatory snack.

What *Ernest* needed was a RuckRaft from Above Below – an inflatable raft that can carry your rucksack and all your gear for a multi day cross-country swim. And when we say it can carry all your gear, we mean it – the raft comes with

a giant drybag, into which you can stuff your tent, sleeping bag, walking boots, food and as many clothes as you need.

The raft can even carry a Brompton on top, should you fancy combining your swim and walk with a stretch of cycling. Manufactured in Britain, the raft is made from strong yet lightweight marine grade fabrics and inflates in 30 seconds.
RuckRaft, £139.99, abovebelow.sc

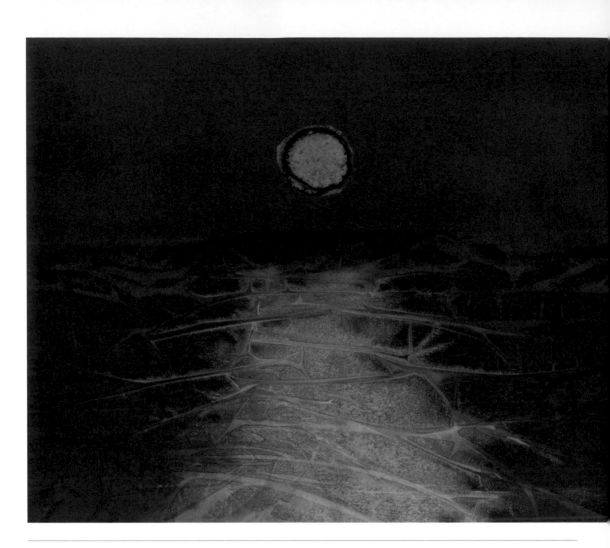

GEAR
TRAIL SOAPS

Trying to reenact the wilds of a coastal pine forest in the shower just doesn't cut it with a bottle of supermarket-own-brand shower gel, does it?

Luckily Wingfield's is on hand with their selection of Juniper Ridge body washes – no nasties or synthetics, all scented with steam-distilled essential oils and saponified organic oils from plants hand-picked on the trail. The liquid is concentrated so a little goes a long way, and the bottles, made from sugarcane, are 100 per cent recyclable.

Choose from four scents: White Sage, Coastal Pine, Cascade Forest and Desert Cedar, and find yourself transported to the Mojave Desert, Eastern Sierras or temperate rainforests of Cascadia.

Juniper Ridge Body Wash; £12.95; wingfields.co.uk

WORKMANSHIP
◀ REIMAGINED LANDSCAPES

During lockdown, artist and photographer Joseph Wright found new ways of capturing landscapes, all the while never venturing further than 10ft from his back door.

How would you describe yourself as an artist?
A visual narrator of inner and outer landscapes. My aims have been to reveal stories of the land and how we inhabit and respond to it, in part, developed through my own lifelong relationship with the countryside and edgelands. I seek to enquire whether our connectedness to nature can be found in the least expected and often neglected places. The places often ignored because of our idealised perception of pastoral landscape.

Has this changed during lockdown?
My objectives remain the same – my fascination and enquiry of the landscape continues unabated. But, while lockdown may have physically hemmed me in, my mind has remained free to wander.

Tell us about *Study of the Landscape*.
The series was born out of a need to stay connected to the environments I was denied access to during lockdown. One of my experiments was to explore physical manipulation of cyanotype materials, and I found I was able to create abstract expressions of landscape forms. These forms constantly shifted as the sun's UV light caused reactions in the sensitiser materials, creating sequences that spanned many days of exposure. These works continue to live and thrive – each time they're exposed to light they morph, albeit less each time – perhaps a metaphor for the virus.
See Joseph's work on Instagram @joearwright

DENDROLOGY
THE WALKING PALM

Native to the tropical rainforests of the Americas, the 'walking palm', *Socratea exorrhiza*, has a curious appearance, with stilt-like roots that lift the body of the tree clear of the ground. Not only do these roots look like a collection of woody legs, but some say the tree can actually use them to walk – rather like a real-life version of the Ents from Tolkien's *The Lord of the Rings*.

The idea is that the walking palm sometimes gets shaded out by other trees and needs to move to a sunnier spot, so it very slowly stretches out new roots, like timber tentacles. Once these have taken hold, the tree allows the roots on the other side to die off, and in this way it makes its ponderous progress across the forest floor at a rate of up to 20 metres a year.

Alas, it appears that in all probability the march of the walking palm – like that of Tolkien's Ents – is the stuff of fiction. While a small number of biologists still believe in it, most experts are confident that despite their leggy appearance, the trees never 'walk' anywhere, and spend their lives rooted in one spot. **Words: Joly Braime, Illustration: Dan Bright.**

EXPLORE
HOW TO LAY &
TRACK A SCOUT TRAIL

Oh, for the halcyon days of scout camp. Living unwashed in a field for a week, playing with knives and fire, trading contraband, subsisting on fry-ups and E-numbers. Veterans of this wholesome experience will probably also have enjoyed the classic scouting game of tracking a trail, where you try to find your way to a secret location by following improvised symbols made from natural materials like twigs and stones.
Words and illustrations: **Joly Braime**

Directions

Arrows constructed out of sticks are the most helpful way to give directions, but less fun for this same reason. Subtler tactics include tying a tuft of grass to point the right way, or placing one rock on top of another then using a third rock to indicate direction. This latter arrangement is particularly difficult to distinguish from any old pile of stones, and has been responsible for many a wild goose chase.

Help and hazards

Show-offs have a wider range of symbols at their disposal, including zig-zags to indicate water, or parallel lines for an obstacle. A generous scout might leave a cache or message for friends on their trail, marked by a square with an arrow coming off it. Sticks or stones placed inside the square indicate the number of paces to the drop – possibly a melted Mars bar or a dog-eared *Point Horror* sealed up in a sandwich bag.

GEAR
◀ SLEEP IN A CLOUD

What's this, a sleeping bag that rolls up into a fluffy pillow, and snaps into a cape for snuggling around the campfire? Why, we at *Ernest* believe the Cloudtouch Blanket to be the sleeping bag of dreams, for not only are they extremely versatile and practical for van life, they also come in a stunning range of designs – we're particularly enamoured with the retro yet contemporary Modadnock Two (*pictured*). Breathable, lightweight, water- and stain-resistant and made from recycled plastic bottles – yep, this blanket gets our eyes-closed-smiling-nod-and-hand-clap. **Voited Cloudtouch Blanket, €129,90, voited.eu**

Gone home
A dot in a circle means that the scout has finished laying his trail and 'gone home', perhaps pausing to enjoy a crafty cig while his companions are hopelessly lost in the woods. This symbol has an extra poignancy for scouters, since it's also a euphemism for death. To this day, if you get an email about an old scout leader with 'gone home' in the subject line, it means their trail is at an end.

AROMACHOLOGY
SCENT OF THE SEA

Wouldn't it be nice if you could somehow bottle the smell of adventure? That salty touch of sun-dried seawater that lingers on your skin like the sand between your toes.

Cornish brand land&water has created a range of bath products, candles and fragrances that aim to provoke those scent memories long after you've returned home. Inspired by the sands of Watergate

Bay on the Atlantic coast, and dreamed up in collaboration with perfumer Richard Howard, founder Pix Ashworth says: "The collection draws on memories of wading out into a river, throwing myself into the sea and walking along coast paths."

Apparently, smells can be a shortcut to memory, so you can douse yourself in their citrus, spice and spike moss body wash during your pre-commute shower, then lose yourself in recollections of surf and sunsets as you swelter behind a face mask on the number 19 bus. Words: **Joly Braime.** landandwater.co.uk

contributors

This edition of *Ernest Journal* was brought to you by a talented troupe of writers, photographers, illustrators, film-makers, oceanographers and aurora chasers.

RUSSELL ARNOTT, oceanographer
As well as researching plankton at the University of Bath, Russell is educational director of Incredible Oceans. He aims to enthuse as many people as possible about the wonders of our oceans. **incredibleoceans.org**

FINN BEALES, photographer and director
Finn is an award-winning travel, lifestyle and commercial photographer. He is known for his cinematic style and the narrative he weaves throughout his work.
madebyfinn.com

OLIVER BERRY, writer and photographer
Oliver is a Cornwall-based writer and photographer that specialises in travel and nature. He has travelled to 69 countries and five continents, but has a particular fascination for far-flung islands. **oliverberry.com**

WILLEM BETTS, writer and photographer
Willem is a slow-moving photographer, writer, and videographer from Canada. When he's at home in British Columbia he spends his days looking for dying trees to run through his sawmill.

JOLY BRAIME, writer and editor
Joly's workload is fairly eclectic, from outdoor magazines and a book on Sherlock Holmes to erotic fiction. He likes tramping the moors and filling his coal shed with homebrew.
jolybraime.co.uk

SAM BREWSTER, illustrator and filmmaker
Sam has worked with *The New York Times*, *The Guardian* and *The Financial Times*, and has illustrated several children's books including *Book of Bones*, published by Phaidon.
sambrewster.com

DAN COOK, photographer
Dan is typically found exploring British landscapes, seeking to capture the feel of the great outdoors through photography. Dan works on commissions and creating fine art prints from his Sheffield studio. **@dan_scape**

REBECCA DOUGLAS, photographer
Rebecca is a photographer, traveller and explorer who adores people and places. You'll most likely find her somewhere subzero, chasing the aurora borealis with a smile.
rebeccadouglas.co.uk

HOLLIE HARMSWORTH, filmmaker and photographer
Based in Conwy, Hollie enjoys hiking up mountains, jumping in lakes or rambling along coastal cliffs. Her work embodies all she loves about the outdoors. **hollieharm.com**

JON HAYWARD,
designer and photographer
Jon lives just outside Snowdonia National Park, where he has developed his passion for photography among the rugged mountains.
jonmhayward.com

SAM HOBSON, photographer
Sam is best known for his wildlife photography. His words and pictures explore the liminal spaces between the man-made and natural worlds, inspiring a deeper connection to nature.
samhobson.co.uk

ADAM HOWLING, illustrator
Adam has illustrated for *The Guardian*, *BBC Music* and *Wired Magazine*, and has also illustrated a *Doctor Who* A-Z children's book, published by Penguin.
adamhowling.com

LUCY JONES, writer
Lucy's writing on nature, science, and culture has been published by BBC Earth, *The Guardian* and *The New Statesman*. Her latest book *Losing Eden: Why Our Minds Need the Wild* was longlisted for the Wainwright Prize.

COLIN NICHOLLS, photographer
Colin is a photographer specialising in weddings and editorial work, with a passion for landscape and street photography. He shoots on a Fuji X100 and Fuji XE1.
colinnichollsphotography.com

JIM MARSDEN, photographer
Jim was born in the Rossendale Valley, Lancashire. He has created work for Hiut Denim, the DO Lectures, Millican and Sawday's alongside his own projects, and teaches for Leica. iamjim.co.uk

AIDAN MEIGHAN, illustrator
Aidan's work is linear, pattern-based and plays with perspective, lending itself to maps and architectural drawings. He explores themes of treehouses, rooftops and imagined landscapes.
whereaboutsmaps.com

DAN RICHARDS, writer
Dan's first book *Holloway* was co-authored with Robert Macfarlane and Stanley Donwood. Other titles include *Climbing Days*, which explores the life of his mountaineering aunt Dorothy Pilley. @Dan_Zep

FERN SCOTT, writer and filmmaker
Fern is a Bristol-based filmmaker whose films are celebrations of creativity. She is drawn to exploring the many ways that being outdoors and in nature benefits our emotional health.
greatscottfilms.com

RUTH THORP, illustrator
Ruth is an illustrator and designer based in Bath. She is inspired by incredible landscapes and the spirit of adventure.
@ruththorpstudio
ruththorpstudio.co.uk

KATE TIGHE, writer
Kate is a writer from northwest England with a specific interest in the science of food. An avid home cook herself, Kate has long been drawn to the 'hows' and 'whys' of the kitchen.
@katetighecooks

MACK WOODRUFF, photographer
Mack is a photographer and cinematographer, specialising in documentaries. Having travelled to more than 60 countries, he has a deep appreciation for the human experience and diverse cultures that inhabit the Earth.

stay in touch...

Subscribe to our newsletter for
more curiosity and slow adventure
ernestjournal.co.uk/newsletter